Stephane Grappelli

'There are artists like quinces, whose
fragrance does not cloy . . .'
      – PALINURUS (*Cyril Connolly*)
    'The Unquiet Grave'

'Improvisation is another form of
composition. It's fresh. Also one must
try to think young in this life.'
        – S. GRAPPELLI, 1981

Stephane Grappelli

or The Violin with Wings

A Profile By

RAYMOND HORRICKS

and selected discography by

TONY MIDDLETON

HIPPOCRENE BOOKS
New York

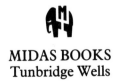

MIDAS BOOKS
Tunbridge Wells

In the same popular music series
Elvis Presley – A Study in Music by Robert Matthew-Walker
Lennon & McCartney by Malcolm Doney
Bob Dylan – From a Hard Rain to a Slow Train by Tim Dowley
    and Barry Dunnage
Frank Sinatra by John Frayn Turner
The Nolans – In the Mood for Stardom by Kim Treasurer
Pink Floyd by Karl Dallas
Blues Off the Record by Paul Oliver
Simon & Garfunkel by Robert Matthew-Walker

First published UK in 1983 by
MIDAS BOOKS
12 Dene Way, Speldhurst
Tunbridge Wells, Kent TN3 0NX

ISBN 0 85936 235 3 (UK)

First published USA in 1983 by
HIPPOCRENE BOOKS INC
171 Madison Avenue
New York, NY 10016

ISBN 0 88254 727 5 (USA)

Printed and bound in Great Britain
at The Pitman Press, Bath

for Roger Lacroix and Georgette
also for Vivienne Leighton and
for my friend Jack Hobbs, the pianist
not the opening bat

Contents

AVANT-PROPOS

AFTER JASCHA HEIFETZ Stephane Grappelli has been our century's most famous and popular violinist.

The fact that he creates jazz music on the violin has now long left behind all the original scorners and doubting Thomases. We have no need to place the word jazz in apologetic inverted commas with regard to the instrument itself. He has given it a credence and a validity and above everything an originality which defy explanation, except just to say 'thank God' certain men and women are put into this life with a yearning either to be heightened individuals or who can recognise and appreciate such abilities in others.

Stephane is unique: a one-off. You can sit outside Florian's in Venice with a half-bottle of the best white wine in Italy and listen to a very adequate jazz violinist play *Sweet Georgia Brown*. On the opposite side of the great square of Saint Mark's from you – albeit faintly – are the sounds of a rival musician playing *Lady Be Good*. But both – I don't know whether for reasons of commercial cunning or simply slavish devotion – will be imitating the style and sound which Grappelli invented and then proceeded to make the most easily recognisable in the entire modern history of the violin. Forget these worldwide imitations though. As with Picasso or Matisse or Ernest Hemingway, there is only the one original. That's really why I call Grappelli unique.

Much the same can be said about his position and reputation. Since the first emergence of jazz in the United States following the blues and ragtime at the beginning of the 1900s, certainly the music has become internationalised. And Europe has made significant contributions to its list of masters. Remarkable talents, as varied and contrasting as Django Reinhardt (whose death was premature); the composer Spike Hughes; Belgium's Bobby Jaspar; bassists Dave Holland and Niels-Henning Ørsted-Pedersen; and Great Britain's best-known piano and guitar exports, George Shearing, Gordon Beck and John McLaughlin. Plus performers like trombonist George Chisholm who have held their own with, and earned the praises of such giants as

1

The audience applauds.

Coleman Hawkins and Benny Carter. Even so: even surrounded by the living or recorded evidence of these considerable men, in his later, more mature years and playing better than ever, Stephane has steadily ascended the ladder of fortune until he is currently regarded as Europe's No. 1 jazz master. He has taken the art of his music where not many others dare to go. And he has done it with an instrument many people spent years telling us was useless as a vehicle for jazz-playing. Perhaps, however, this is the next important thing to be said about him. So many men are born and grow up to a destiny of being faced by

2

barriers of one kind or another. A precious few have had the nerve and the will-power to leap or vault over them.

Meanwhile the man himself has been a near miracle of self-preservation. Admittedly he's paced himself. But watch him come on stage at the Royal Albert Hall or play a set at Ronnie Scott's; sit only a couple of tables away from him with a coffee or a glass of *rosé* during the Nice Jazz Festival. You have to remind yourself that he's still human. To be that good, I mean, and yet keep up the punishing work-schedule he does. Okay – so he feels the cold and doesn't like the winter. He usually spends from January to March at his flat near the sea at Cannes. Don't forget though that he then devotes the other nine months of the year to making his living as a *fêted*, but nevertheless itinerant performer, commuting between Tokyo and New York City and Edinburgh and San Francisco. Just once in a while – but sometimes only once in a year – he is able to sip an *apéritif* in his native Paris with the knowledge that he has the rest of the evening to himself. It definitely doesn't happen very often. Because Mister Grappelli travels his artistry. He may now (at last) be properly paid for his services. All the same, his personal life remains less a style than a course of identikit hotel-bedrooms, the numbing nightcap and the first onset of sleep well after midnight. In fact, although it's true that when I say his violin has 'wings' I'm referring to the beautiful, soaring quality of his playing, I have to add that it literally does have wings. Big silver ones, which it rests inside. Stephane would have difficulty counting all the hours he's spent airborne during the last ten years.

That he isn't often heard to complain is simply another measure of the man. Fate, he believes, has taken him into music and into music as a way of communicating with the thousands and tens of thousands who hand over money to listen to him play. It's a matter of personal pride therefore that he's never ever let them down.

3

Chapter ONE

THIS COMPARATIVELY short book is not a formal biography of Stephane Grappelli. Instead it has become one writer's attempt to view the man and his art from more than just the different points in their chronology. For I find there is an almost diamond-like quality about Stephane's music making – and a quality gem, in common with the truth itself, offers many facets. In private conversation he rarely reminisces. He lives for the present and enjoys it. Each day, he considers, is the high tide of our individual existence. Consequently why keep looking back? As he says, think young, and of now, here.

If some of my angle shots of him are unconventional then I hope at least they are also revealing. For the great jazz masters are themselves unconventional. That's what makes them so interesting, and why their creativity is both surprising and so easy to identify. Impossible to mistake the sound and phrasing of Louis Armstrong and Sidney Bechet, of Charlie Parker and Dizzy Gillespie. But no-one ever knows *what* they're going to play before they play it. Again that is how improvisation becomes composition. Because it is the product of a mind which deliberately avoids the ordinary, and dogma and all that comes out glibly. Jazz is the result of the way you think and feel and then play, not something to be confected beforehand or have rules of the game applied to it.

Which in turn reminds me of a Zen teacher during the Meiji era (1868-1912), Nan-in. One day he received a Japanese university professor who demanded to know about Zen. Nan-in served him tea. He poured the visitor's cup full, and then kept pouring. The professor watched the overflow until he could no longer restrain himself. 'It's already full,' he cried. 'No more will go in!' 'Like the cup,' Nan-in said, 'you are full of your own opinions and speculations. How can I show you Zen unless you first empty your cup?'

Similarly jazz is very much the man who keeps an open mind, a window on the roads through life. It's also how he is, what makes him tick. Consequently I've tried to discover about Stephane from other than just printed sources and the recorded evidence; and especially via the eyes and ears of several of the musicians who've actually worked with him and travelled in his company.

I may have made mistakes of course, but certainly not the one of taking my subject for granted. And meanwhile what I've learned has if anything increased the fascination first felt for his music on that red-letter day when at the age of fourteen I purchased – for four shillings and eight old pence – my initial 78 rpm record by the Quintet of the Hot Club.

To begin with though, before going into any of the facts about Stephane's life, I decided to ask another string player about him – and specifically one I could rely on to be objective.

John Meek teaches the violin, is currently principal viola with the English National Opera, and I date my friendship with him from what might easily have begun as a row. When, starting out as a record producer with Decca, I took charge of my first big orchestral session he glared at me – rightly, given the benefit of hindsight – because in the emergency of sorting out copying mistakes in the band parts I'd put off his request to change the temperature in the studio. I should explain: prior to this I'd studied the piano (and fooled around with various brass instruments). But I'd never played a member of the violin family, and later, during the tea-break, he explained to me how the gut-'devils' are far more susceptible to a room's heating and cooling than the brass or woodwind. I digested the lesson, but it also led to an association which has included my respect for his judgement and knowledge of the history of stringed instruments. Also, he's an admirer of Grappelli. But this would never blinker him; as I believe the following illustrates. He writes:

'Thinking again about the career and life style of Stephane, I realise that my admiration for his playing is matched by astonishment at his ability to retain and utilise his startling talents into comparative old age. In this respect he has been equalled by very few violinists of distinction – although it has been justly claimed that the long and prominent working life of Arnold Rosè (1863-1946) would be difficult to supersede. I heard Rosè playing a concert of string quartets at London's Wigmore Hall in 1942. Then in his seventy-ninth year, he was still a performer of great character, with his intonation the only weakness, due to his becoming slightly deaf. He had been appointed solo violin to the Vienna Opera when only sixteen years old and began his quartet career around the same time. To be capable, sixty-three years later, of publicly presenting such demanding music is a remarkable achievement.

'Conversely, the famous violin pedagogue Carl Flesch tells us in his memoirs of witnessing the early decline in technical ability of two of the most eminent violinists of all time, Eugene Ysaÿe (1858-1931) and Josef Joachim (1831-1907). After the age of about fifty both these men developed faults which inhibited their performances. In the case of Ysaÿe we're told how a trembling bow-arm troubled him so much that he became neurotic about it and this finally drove him from a solo career into conducting and composition. Joachim, an equally outstanding violinist to begin with, suffered similarly – but Flesch is kinder in assuming he was too busy with his other, diverse musical activities to have had sufficient time for regular practice.

'Which is another thing about Stephane Grappelli. With the concert and travel schedule of a leading modern artist, it's hard to imagine that he gets all that much time for practice. Yet he continues to play in a seemingly imperturbable manner. . .'

John goes on:

'It's interesting to ask whether the demands on the nervous and physical resources of the orthodox artist are greater. And if so, why?

'If a jazz artist can adjust technique to mood and inclination and eschew difficulties which cannot adequately he surmounted at a given moment, then in the long run it would appear that nervous and physical demands will be kept to a reasonable level. Which doesn't detract in the slightest from the genius displayed by Grappelli, who is in a class all by himself.

'Nevertheless, the orthodox soloist has, regardless of mood and feeling, to cope with the usual octaves, tenths, double harmonics and bowing difficulties with absolutely no escape routes. He is trapped by the printed note. To make life even more hazardous, the audience will frequently know the music as intimately as the soloist – and also, possibly, the pitfalls.

'Youth and into early middle age are generally considered to be the period in life when the violinist's situation is more easily handled. And concert artists will disagree, if honest, with the commonly held belief that performing becomes easier with maturity and age. They frequently do become neurotic about the music to be performed, a fate which can be avoided by the jazz player who has so much more freedom of choice in what he actually does.

'Jacques Thibaud, born in 1880 and perhaps the most revered of all French concert violinists, was an artist who insisted on following his own instincts. His became a talent which treated music as a vehicle for self-expression, and in this he may have been closer to the jazz idiom than is generally realised. In striving to overcome the restrictions imposed by the printed note he would cover, and at times even swamp the music with his own personality. So, eventually perhaps, Stephane Grappelli and Thibaud will be remembered not only as two of France's greatest violinists, but beyond that for their ability to communicate a message of spiritual freedom through music in a diametrically opposite manner.'

John Meek also reminded me that the great Heifetz cancelled his last London concert in the 1960s and had then retired from public performances because he feared that with age some signs of deterioration in his fabulous technique might begin to come through. Which jogged my own memory about how Heifetz often appeared frustrated by the standard violin repertoire. He didn't actually press on to try to be a jazz musician, but he rearranged pieces written for other instruments to test his abilities in different ways. Albéniz's *Sevilla*, Op.47, for instance, comes from the piano suite 'Española'. Rearranged by Heifetz it is brilliant, but fiendishly difficult for any other violinist to play. He also commissioned and then helped revise the score of Sir William Walton's Violin Concerto, and like Fritz Kreisler, experimented with folk songs and popular novelty numbers, possibly because he shared Kreisler's belief that 'joy, sadness, fear, anger, can all be projected from one heart directly into another through the medium of music. This is because music is the most direct and untrammelled exponent of human emotion.'

Stephane Grappelli's playing echoes such sentiments. In the art of communication he has to be regarded as the peer of these grand concert violinists. In contrast though, having started out as a classical student, he then found an inspiration in jazz which gave him a true vocation and led to the creation of his very individual style. (Although one is provided with an example of his musical beginnings whenever he decides to improvise on a theme by Bach.)

Nowadays his music has turned Stephane into a citizen of the

First look at a new score.

world. In every other respect, however, it is hard to conceive of his being anything except a French national. It's the surname which is the giveaway: on his father's side the violinist comes of Italian extraction. (Originally the Grappelli ended in a *y*.) No matter. He was born in Paris and grew up to be as French as the Cardin scarves and multi-coloured shirts he favours.

He was born under the sign of Aquarius: on 26 January, 1908. In the view of critic Frank Tenot, Grappelli the stylist is 'a sensitive and refined musician who is both a sentimentalist and an artist. He likes elegant, well-balanced and melodic phrases and his improvisations are constructed with the logic of a person who thinks clearly and knows exactly where he wants to go.' Well, if the style is also the man, then the family unit must be taken into consideration. The first relevant point here being that his mother died when he was only three.

His father was an aspiring dancer who later tried his hand at commerce (not very successfully); and Stephane would face a long, long haul before he made it to the top – including being put into an

8

The Grappelli concentration.

orphanage for a time because his father couldn't cope, financially or as substitute mother. On the other hand he revered education, the senior Grappelli, and he had good taste: which gave the boy a start. Today the violinist is noted for his diverse interests and sophistication; and at the outset it is likely that both these were sparked in some measure by his father. Even more important, the latter had convinced musical ambitions on his son's behalf, so that when Steph responded and displayed a natural ability the father saw to it he gained every encouragement. And specifically by taking him along to the advanced and controversial school of Isadora Duncan: who despite his being poor agreed to take him for lessons in music and dance.

'I had my first violin at the age of twelve,' he recalls. 'A three-quarter size, bought just around the corner in the Rue Rochechouart. All the way home I hugged it so hard I almost broke it!' He is specific about being turned on to music by the time he was six. 'It was hearing Debussy's *Prélude À L'Après-midi D'un Faune* based on the Mallarmé poem. So, so beautiful. My father thought I should go in for ballet, but after this, deep down, I knew I wanted

'I think that was a good take!'

to play. The First World War got in the way of things. I had to stay in an awful *pension* for a while because my father was called to the front. There was no opportunity to have an instrument to practise there. But once I had the violin I worked at it that much harder.'

Stephane grew up therefore to be a thoroughly trained musician, the result of dedication, the Duncan school, private practice with his father (they studied *solfeggio* together) and finally classes at the Conservatoire. He had gone deeply into the theory and history of music, knew many classicial works by heart and was a fast and excellent reader. His chosen instruments were the violin and also the piano.

Actually not enough has been made of Stephane's abilities as a pianist. When he sits down and plays the classics he evidences a firm technique and a beautiful gradation of touch. Meanwhile as a jazz piano-player he can be quite formidable. His stated preferences here have been Bix Beiderbecke (especially on *In A Mist*) and above all Art Tatum. But he is also perfectly at home rolling out solos which evoke Fats Waller and the Harlem stride-men. The thing is, he nearly always keeps this 'other' ability hidden from his public. He likes to relax at the piano and just play for his friends. Max

Harris, who wrote all the arrangements for the early Grappelli-Menuhin records, listened with surprise and delight when at the end of their first session Stephane moved to the keyboard and entertained everyone with ten minutes of neo-Waller. After this, the other musicians involved could hardly wait for the Frenchman 'to do a little Fats'.

Stephane can be heard on piano accompanying Django Reinhardt through a version of *Sweet Georgia Brown* on 'The Legendary Django' LP (once available on His Master's Voice CLP1890 but now a sought-after collectors' item). Following this though his talent was mostly kept under wraps as regards recording until the marvellous 'Young Django' sessions of 19-21 January, 1979 for MPS (LP 0068-230). For the last of these dates the American guitarist Larry Coryell had contributed the theme *Blues For Django And Stephane*. And after the violinist had relinquished his bow he was persuaded to play a piano solo. The result is one of the most exciting tracks he has ever laid down. He commences with the kind of delicacy and balance normally associated with a Teddy Wilson or Mel Powell. But then suddenly the left-hand thunders out and by the end it's all Waller, James P. Johnson and the kings of boogie-woogie.

However: at the beginning it was a question of how to make a living. He was bright, he was highly articulate and he undoubtedly possessed a great gift. But he had been born without the proverbial silver spoon. Since then his father had shown affection and provided what he could towards his studies. Now it was up to him. For a couple of months he stood outside a hotel and lived off the tips from opening taxi-doors.

To a degree the way ahead appeared simple and clear, because by the end of his musical training, like many Europeans Stephane had fallen under the spell of American jazz and dance bands, particularly once he'd heard the first recordings by violinist Joe Venuti. 'I was fifteen, working as part-time pianist in a cinema when I first heard jazz. It was the tunes to begin with, *Lady Be Good* and *Tea For Two*. I can't explain, but I responded. I found I could improvise.' He also recalls the first disc he ever heard of the music: *Stumbling* by the Mitchell Jazz Kings; and of listening through the keyhole of a nightclub-door to some band playing *Hot Lips*. 'But then of course, later, I heard Joe. When I was 18/19. Eddie South I didn't hear until 1937.'

11

Joe Venuti.

Venuti (oddly enough another Italian, born at Lecco) was only a few years senior to Grappelli, but already a star on the US scene. He was the pioneer of his instrument in jazz, attacking the melodic lines with a fiery swing and improvising some dazzling runs and variations. Stephane was mesmerised by what he heard; then wildly enthusiastic about the new music. After briefly experimenting he was thrilled to discover he could play in the same way. It was just like a duck taking to water. '*This,*' he informed his somewhat startled, but afterwards acquiescent father, 'is the music I want to play. I can think in the idiom and I can feel it. Jazz is the sound of today, and tomorrow. It has liberty – one can invent within it!'

The next several years were all hard slog. 'At this period it wasn't all that easy to play the violin for dancing.' At first people laughed at the things he created – and even many jazz *aficionados* shook their heads. Venuti was a flash in the pan, they said. The violin had no chance of making it as a regular part of the music.

However, the young Grappelli persevered and joined the overall scuffle for work in the capital. Miserable jobs they were to begin with; a case of taking anything that was going. Often they meant rough and evil-smelling *cafés* where no one took any notice of the faded posters stating the law against drunkenness. Payment would be a handful of francs and a glass or two of harsh red wine.

Worse was to come. Sometimes he would land a decent gig with a band, notably Gregor and His Gregorians. And once he got a trip to the South of France, to Nice playing as one of two pianists with the casino orchestra. Sometimes too he would still be booked to do a cinema; six hours of ragtime, Mozart and straining his neck to follow what was happening on the flickering screen. Then *The Jazz Singer* arrived; the first talkie. 'I didn't like it on principle. It put me out of a job!'

Very occasionally there'd be a respectable tea-dance. While on yet another occasion he had to borrow a saxophone and pretend to be able to play it in addition to violin because a certain lady club-owner wanted that particular double. 'I took one lesson and got through an appalling version of *Nola*,' he told Len Skeat.

Gradually though even the bad *café* nights began to elude him. The Depression had affected France as well; economic recovery would prove to be slow. By the end of the 1920s Stephane found himself out on the streets, busking.

Grappelli smiles ruefully at the mere mention of those days. He'd be out in all weathers, wrapped in a big heavy overcoat with pockets the size of panniers, tramping between boulevards and the city's squares, pausing to play, waiting for some small reward, then moving on. Or he might entertain a picture palace queue. At times, after he had paid for a sandwich and a *café crème* the most he went back with could be totted up in *sous*.

Luxury was every once in a while going to the Paris Coliseum where the Mitchell Jazz Kings played, still the 'in' group at this period and one of the lucky few with a regular job. Other times though he slept rough; and once, according to Alan Clare, for several weeks at the house of a terrible old harridan, a great big mansion really, but cold as the Arctic and as if filled with a mob of ghosts. (His father had disappeared somewhere on a 'business' venture.) Moreover, as he also told Alan Clare, you had to expect the unexpected and a few hazards. For example, much of the Parisian population is housed in tenement buildings designed by

(Photo from 'Jazz Away From Home')

Gregor and His Gregorians, 1930. Stephane is fifth from right, his friend
Philippe Brun extreme right.

Baron Haussmann under the rule of Napoleon III. With elaborate
ironwork balconies, they are usually of five or six storeys, each with
its own social stratum. The rich occupy the first-floor apartments
with the poorest inhabitants at the very top. 'But the poor were the
generous ones,' the violinist stressed. 'And franc-pieces tossed
down from that height could cut your head open! Or damage your
finger. You had to keep looking up when you played to see if any
windows were being opened. The rich on the other hand only threw
you coins if they didn't like the music and wanted you to push
off. . .' Without this taste of busking however his future life would
certainly have been a good deal different. For fate was about to deal
him a hand which even the intuitive Stephane could hardly have
anticipated.

It was nothing less than bizarre, the first meeting between
Stephane, suave, educated but down-and-out, and the scruffy,

semi-illiterate Belgian guitarist, Django. Also, without divine intervention it was something like a million-to-one chance. 'We played in a courtyard,' Steph tells us. 'People were throwing money out of the windows. Django and his Gypsies wanted to play in the yard. We argued. We almost had a fight. That's how we got to know each other. It was in the late 'twenties.'

Chapter TWO

His sound was ambulant and saintly. And his rhythms were his own as the stripes of a tiger, as his phosphorescence and his moustache. He lived within his skin. He rendered it royal and invisible to the hunter.
— JEAN COCTEAU *about* DJANGO

DJANGO REINHARDT (1910-1953). Impossible to conceive of a man more alien to the basic nature of Grappelli. Whereas the latter had evolved as someone quick, responsible and given a break one of the ultimate professionals, the Belgian gypsy could claim to be a poetic musical genius – but not much else. Sloppy, almost incapable of getting up before midday, a spendthrift and a compulsive itinerant, Django's eccentric behaviour and life style

Django's caravan.

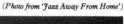

(Photo from 'Jazz Away From Home')

(Photo from 'Jazz Away From Home')

His damaged hand.

would at times test their relationship to its absolute limits. But they had a love of jazz in common and eventually, with their group and over a number of years, the formula for success.

Marginally younger than Grappelli – although likewise an Aquarian – Jean-Baptiste 'Django' Reinhardt was born close to the border with France, at Liverchies, near Charleroi, on 23 January, 1910. His family were part of a *troupe* of comedians, almost always on the move and therefore his schooling was patchy, with his further skipping classes and a cheeky rebelliousness orchestrated by family beatings and, at the different schools he half-attended, fairly regular caning. As a result, music became his principal diversion and consolation. He too tested his fingers with violin and bow – a natural choice for a Romany – before switching to the banjo and finally guitar. (Critic Daniel Halperin recalls hearing him play someone else's fiddle at a party in the 1940s. 'He had some jazz feeling on the instrument, but for the most part he played it with much *schmaltz,* and what is known in Yiddish as *krechtzing,* a throbbing, minor-key wailing with Hebraic chants. But maybe Django was just kidding around; it was hard to know when he was and when he wasn't.')

However, on the night of 2 November 1928 there occurred the event which nearly took his life but instead turned him into something special, another musical one-off. Already a chain-smoker, he ignited his wife's cooking-oil, and in the fire which ensued both the caravan and his two guitars were destroyed. He himself sustained injuries that would keep him in hospital for nearly a year. And – of freakish significance – two fingers of his left (the fingering) hand were permanently paralysed.

17

Until the fire Django, an avid jazz fan, had been scratching a living playing slavish imitations of what was coming from America. He might even have become the European equivalent of Eddie Lang. Now though, and refusing to be beaten, he managed to put his small finger on the E string, the next on the B and set about developing an entirely new technique on the guitar. Based on very nimble, single-note picking and with certain passages played in octaves, using the flesh at the base of the thumb to make the second line, he found quite quickly that he had arrived at something truly exciting. A style of obvious originality, and one which would make him, a few years later, the first European player to have an important influence on American jazz. Its effectiveness was added to by drawing upon his own gypsy roots as well as jazz sources. In accompanying another soloist he always played with a great sense of timing and swing. But within his own solos he let the imagination run free. Often the outcome would be rhapsodic, even romantic; but it was also much more melodic, with longer lines and a far wider variety of phrases. Add to this his growing powers as a composer and one has some idea of the 'lyrical' side to Django which won the admiration of Jean Cocteau, Pablo Picasso and other leading artists and intellectuals. As regards jazz though, then the music would

(Photo from 'Jazz Away From Home')

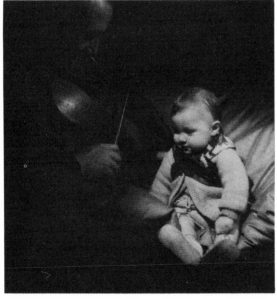

The guitarist plays a violin for his son.

have to wait for the advent of Charlie Christian before knowing a guitarist as revolutionary.

To take up the story again, Django's hospitalisation confirms that his first, crucial meeting with Grappelli must have taken place towards the end of 1929. And certainly by the end of the following year they were seeing a lot of one another. Soon it was not just a matter of sharing pitches. They began to sit down and actually work out ideas together. Ideas which enabled them to play duets. For Stephane was also now fashioning an original style – and of an originality which seemed suited to go with Django's. They even planned to co-compose several things. . .

Prior to this, although adept on his instrument, Stephane had remained essentially a copyist of Joe Venuti. His principal admiration in jazz was for Louis Armstrong, the No.1 virtuoso – and sometimes he endeavoured to translate 'Satchmo'-like phrases on the violin. But through the 1920s Venuti was the true pacesetter. Given time other outstanding American jazz violinists would emerge: Eddie South, Stuff Smith, Ray Nance (an underrated player) and in the 1960s 'free jazz' doyen Ornette Coleman began to experiment with it. But beyond any dispute, and before the change to individuality in Grappelli, Venuti gave jazz violin its initial style and vocabulary. Only he had broken the instrument's Cinderella-image.

In moving away from Venuti, at first Stephane had to plough a very lonely furrow indeed. He was determined to be his own man though, particularly with the fine example of Django around, and he too began to combine a more romantic and sophisticated approach to melody with the underlying swing. Venuti tended to improvise short, tough, on-the-beat phrases. The now-maturing Grappelli became the more inventive soloist of the two because he was the more daring. His style was more flowing and (as with Django) his lines came to be very elastic and extended. Naturally the romantic aspect came out more strongly in performing ballads. But on up-tempo numbers too his agile brain enabled him to think ahead, to conceive improvised ideas or variations on a given melody and its set of chords which gave his solos a consistently logical development. In the true and later Grappelli only the feeling of swing reconnects our minds with Venuti. The playing and types of idea are quite different, as neat and yet beguiling as the Rubik cube. In the 1940s, Stephane cleverly modified this style to take account of be-bop, but otherwise it has served him remarkably well through to the present day. As well as permitting him to fit in with a bewildering assortment of other jazzmen. Stephane Grappelli with Kenny Clarke, with Roland Hanna and Larry Coryell? It just didn't seem possible. Then it actually happened.

Two further qualities need to be included in any discussion of Stephane's style. One is the clearness and purity of his tone. Venuti's tone can be harsh and rasping. Similarly Stuff Smith's and Ray Nance's – although Stuff makes up for it by playing with true 'balls', while Ray Nance always has his humour to fall back on. In contrast the Grappelli tone has a classical beauty, his gift to jazz from all his early training. It doesn't matter how fast he's playing. And it isn't sweet; simply pure. The other thing is his musical memory, still infallible past the age of seventy. Just a select group of leading jazzmen (Milt Jackson, Stan Getz, a few more) give the impression of being able to reprise every tune they've ever heard. Also, as Woody Herman pointed out about Milt Jackson, the *whole* tune – the chords, the middle-eight, the resolve. Stephane belongs with this group. His accurate knowledge of standard songs and jazz works is tremendous.

Back to the association with Django though . . .

STEPHANE (to Len Skeat): 'It was a love-hate relationship really. He could be very moody and jealous – and sometimes stubborn just to prove his own importance. I remember when we first came to England, for instance. I had some English by then, Django none. In any case I handled all our business because usually he didn't want to be bothered. So I okayed the contract and was about to sign it when suddenly he jabbed his finger down, and said: *I don't agree with this clause.* So I translated it. It guaranteed us first-class travel! Then again, I'd get mad at his lateness. I'm fanatical about punctuality. But every so often, if he felt like it, he'd wander off into the country, dabble with paints or go fishing. I'd be left to make the excuses.'

Nevertheless they struck sparks off each other creatively. Often too Django would return from his fishing-rods with a marvellous idea, the theme of a *Nuages* or *Manoir De Mes Rêves*. And then it was always Stephane he went looking for to approve it. Stephane again: 'In 1931 I was playing at this club in Montparnasse. Suddenly I saw a dark face staring at me with great intensity. At first I couldn't make out who it was. I can tell you it made me nervous. I thought he was a gangster who didn't like my music!'

Once into the 1930s the work situation started to improve; while Stephane himself began to gain acceptance in jazz circles. His friends were the pianist Stéphane Mougin, also Leon Vauchant and Philippe Brun. Django began to work more or less regularly – for him – with André Ekyan's band. Steph landed a job at the Croix du Sud along the Champs-Elysées. In 1933 both men ended up in the same band at Claridges. Their collaboration, partnership, call it what you will, began to take on a new look.

It was all done backstage, of course. But now they weren't just doing it for fun or picking up each other's ideas. Now they practised together for real, shaping and developing a most imaginative interplay between their two instruments: at once complex and precise, swinging and free sounding. At the same time too their writing took off. Django, the wind properly in his sails, even regularised the fishing to genuine days-off. The result was a

The Quintet of the Hot Club of France.

(Photo from 'Jazz Away From Home')

series of 'classic' jazz pieces by a European artist: the aforesaid *Nuages* and *Manoir De Mes Rêves* (Django's Castle), but continuing with *Daphne, Lentement Mademoiselle, Melodie Au Crépuscule, Enchantment, Danse Nuptiale, Water Lilies, Big Gino* and several simply called *Improvisation* and numbered. With Stephane he composed *Djangology, Sweet Chorus, Minor Swing, Are You In The Mood?, Tears* (probably the best and still the most modern-sounding of their themes), *Swing Guitars* and *Oriental Shuffle*. Moreover Claridges also brought them work in other fields, i.e. accompanying two of France's newest popular singing stars, Jean Sablon and Charles Trenet.

So there they were, for once on a good salary, noticed by Parisian socialites, talked about by the jazz fans – and only a short step from international fame. For when it happened it happened quickly. One evening during the break at Claridges, Django's brother Joseph stopped by and accompanied their impromptus on rhythm guitar. Pierre Nourry, a jazz buff and something of an *entrepreneur* suggested they made it a group and played a concert, to which he then invited France's first and foremost jazz critics, Hugues Panassié and Charles Delaunay. The concert itself was a success; the critics were sufficiently impressed to turn it into the official band of their 'Hot Club', augmented by Roger Chaput (guitar) and Louis Vola (bass). It became known in somewhat cumbersome terms as the Quintet of the Hot Club of France. But cumbersome musically it most certainly was not, as their appearances at Bricktop's showed. Stephane was fully formed as a soloist now, leading off with some of the most brilliant improvisations yet heard from a jazz violinist. Django on featured guitar was equally impressive, and if anything even more startling. In the words of Danny Halperin, 'when he played his left hand was like a bird's claw, greyish brown, with the fingers bunched together like the top half of a question mark.'

'Theirs was an instant triumph,' he goes on. 'With Reinhardt and Grappelli soloing over the guitars-bass rhythm section, the quintet's sound was strong, integrated and compelling – one of the most satisfying sounds in the history of jazz.' Soon they were broadcasting, making records for the newly-formed Ultraphone label and they had as much work as they could handle. But probably their most significant breakthrough came from 1935 onwards once the Americans became aware of them. Both Django

(Photo from 'Jazz Away From Home')

Their first publicity photograph.

and Stephane recorded as part of Coleman Hawkins' All-Star Jam Band (Benny Carter, André Ekyan, Alix Combelle – and Stephane coaxed back onto piano); and these discs together with their own Hot Club releases persuaded the jazz heartland that Europe had at last produced something quite extraordinary. After all their separate years of struggle it now became a question of what to turn down. Apart from records, London would have to wait until 1939 to benefit from the full impact of them. (At the Palladium they shared the bill with Tom Mix, who took his meals with his horse.)

One general point should be made here – but one of particular importance in view of Stephane Grappelli's pre-eminence in the jazz world today. In the heyday of the Quintet of the Hot Club of France, to people at large – which meant the hundreds of thousands who bought their records or saw them 'live' – Stephane and Django, or Django and Stephane, it didn't matter in which order the names came, were equal leaders. But to the 'inside' people of jazz, the real *aficionados*, Django had the edge over Stephane. Especially in America. Time – but also a very long time – has seen a big revision of this estimation. In the 'thirties and 'forties though, Django to the Americans was IT. Mainly, I think, this was because the guitar itself had become more important to jazz than the violin, and Django showed them how the instrument didn't have to be just a rhythmic prop but could play interesting solos like a trumpet, trombone and the saxophone family. By comparison the violin continued to be treated as a novelty element.

Django came to be regarded as an influential master by a whole new generation of guitarists with solo ambitions – by Barney Kessel, Herb Ellis, Tal Farlow, Remo Palmieri, Mundell Lowe, Joe Pass, Kenny Burrell and, not surprisingly, by another largely self-taught virtuoso, Wes Montgomery. All of these and many other players grew up with one ear open to Charlie Christian, his amplifier and his be-bop lines, the other to Django's initial liberation of the picking finger. Again I believe because of the instrument he played, Stephane's artistry was widely but never quite so highly regarded.

Their success affected the two men in entirely different ways. On the surface it hardly appeared to change Django at all. He stayed as dishevelled and crumple-suited as ever; with the same straggly moustache and a *Gauloise* always drooping from his lips. Introverted, brooding, basically good-humoured but sometimes

(Photo from 'Jazz Away From Home')

On the balcony of Pierre Nourry's home in Paris. Left to right: Louis Vola, Django Reinhardt, Stephane, Roger Chaput, Joseph Reinhardt, Jerry Mengo, unknown lady, Charles Delaunay.

sulky, he still preferred his caravan to living in a building. When amused or excited his face lit up. Otherwise he seemed much more interested in composing or his fishing than in people. Also, no matter how much money he earned his pockets were invariably empty. Where had it all gone, his friends asked? He couldn't remember. Although married, he indulged in casual affairs and didn't remember much about them either. Probably because he liked to hit the bottle both before and after a gig.

Contrast this with the new life style of Stephane – sharp, smart and at last able to indulge in the things he had been educated to know but never previously to have. He began to put money aside, to have a savings account. At the same time he went to the best tailors, moved about in society, his furnished apartment evidenced a growing passion for collecting antiques, and without ever seeming to put on weight he displayed a great capacity for eating and

After the show. Relaxation.

drinking. All of these personal traits are still a feature of the Grappelli we admire today, except that in the interests of health he drinks less. More about his sartorial and 'collecting' pursuits later, but a few words here about Stephane the *gourmet* and imbiber.

LEN SKEAT: 'Yes, he certainly likes his food, and he's a great expert on what to order. He prefers a relaxed meal after the show – and when he's in an isolated place there's always a to-do if the hotel staff have betrayed him and closed down the kitchen. Another thing. Although knowledgeable about *haute cuisine,* he's got a terrific weakness for English breakfasts: eggs, bacon, sausages, the lot. And not just at breakfast-time. Four o'clock in the afternoon will do. Also, when you eat with him nobody's food is safe. If there's any delay in bringing his own order, then he'll start looking over at what's on everybody else's plates. Suddenly his fork will strike across like a trident and you'll find the tastiest mouthful has gone. I remember once on the Australian tour we were taken to a marvellous fish restaurant down by Sydney harbour. Stephane had helped himself to most of my seafood salad by the time his lobster came. I wasn't offered any of the lobster.'

Apart from wine with his meals the violinist's favourite tipple is Scotch, single malts if possible. He doesn't smoke, but as his present manager Ed Baxter says, 'he always has a wee drop before playing to warm up the blood'. However this is in moderation. The earlier Grappelli drank a lot more heavily, but rarely showed it. He told Alan Clare about one late-night party he was at with Hermione Gingold: 'After we'd downed all the booze there was in the place I still wasn't drunk, so we finished off her Chanel No.5. . .'

At the Hot Club of France, 1934. Left to right: Rex Stewart, Django, Duke Ellington, Louis Vola.

Outside their playing and composing and the odd jam session he didn't mix much with Django. Their interests kept them apart. In any case, the more fashionable Parisians who liked jazz, and who delighted in having the witty, urbane Grappelli at their cocktail parties, were apprehensive about asking Django along. Even if they did he seldom turned up. Recording sessions too were a hazard. STEPHANE: 'Because Django was always so late. In those days there was no such thing as tape. We had the big master-waxes, the *crêpes suzettes*. You just couldn't afford to make mistakes. But getting Django up for rehearsals was almost impossible. It made recordings worrying events.' But the Quintet itself went from strength to strength – until the outbreak of World War II. When hostilities were declared in 1939 the group had again arrived in London. Flattered, fêted, with money and praises showered upon them they were at the zenith of their popular appeal. Then Hitler moved, and like a bubble bursting their individual fortunes would dissolve into thin air.

After the heady excitement of the British tour they were booked to go on to play in India and Australasia. The war not only put paid to their travelling there, it broke up the group. With the collapse of France and defeat of the British Expeditionary Force in 1940 Stephane, an outspoken anti-Nazi, determined to stay on in Britain. Django was also anti-Nazi, but when he had his first taste of the London blackout and the sirens he decided to take a boat back to France, come what may.

How exactly the guitarist survived the war years, roaming around France and Belgium, keeping a low profile, often being paid little more than the cost of a black market meal, is a jazz fable still not fully explained. For as anyone who has read *Mein Kampf* knows, the gypsies were as much an objective of Hitler's purges as the Europeans of Jewish extraction. Admittedly there were fewer of them; but they were exterminated just as ruthlessly. My own theory is that it was deliberate policy to leave Django alone. (Or at least for as long as he did nothing provocative.) I say this because the Nazis could be remarkably pragmatic when it suited them. The Jewish doctor who took care of Goering's wound following the abortive Munich *putsch* of 1923 was spared; likewise Alfred Rosenberg's mistress. Reinhard Heydrich, the *gauleiter* of Prague and at one time considered Hitler's likely successor was rumoured to have Jewish blood; while Field-Marshal Erich von Manstein, whose plan to circumvent the Maginot Line was adopted by Hitler and smashed the Allies, and who later overran the Crimea, definitely did. It took the great English writer Richard Hughes to shake me over what had been until then an agreeable lunch with the truth that, Goebbels apart, the main Nazi hierarchy was in fact Southern Catholic. I was born a Catholic. (He also insisted that Hitler escapes the historian for the novelist. And certainly his own novel, *The Fox In The Attic* includes the only convincing portrait of Hitler I have read so far.)

Django was a gypsy, true. But he was at the same time a symbol and a cult-figure. The more influential collaborators would have advised their German allies of this. Also, as the columnist Walter Goodman points out: 'It was a muddled time; there were collaborationist *cafés* and resister *cafés*, and you couldn't always predict who would move from ideas to action – or in which direction.' It was the Nazi way to remove their victims quietly (albeit *en masse*); not to take someone the news of whose arrest might provoke widespread civil insurrection in France when their own attentions were firmly focussed upon the east and Russia. Vichy's policy was much the same. Subtle and deadly; but practical. Anyway, Django stayed out of the limelight, did nothing provocative and managed to come through it all.

One other possibility, according to Alan Clare, is that the guitarist made good use of his knowledge of the Paris catacombs – where he'd sometimes practised before the war, and where, literally under the skin of the capital, he could find his way along tunnels the Germans never ventured down. They were a favourite retreat for many gypsies and *clochards* as well as the organised Resistance whenever the heat was on. . .

Because Django's limited future would be bound up with Stephane's only intermittently, except as an influence and in the violinist's memory-bank, perhaps this is the most suitable point to summarise it. Towards the end of the war he had made it back to Paris leading a Quintet which featured clarinettist Hubert Rostaing in place of Stephane. It was not an equivalent success. But in American eyes he was still Europe's most important jazz musician. His concert at the Salle Pleyel on 16 December, 1945 backed by the US Air Transport Command Band was a sell-out and the following year Duke Ellington invited him to go on a coast-to-coast American and Canadian tour. This ought to have been the ultimate success, instead of which, as far as Django was concerned it flopped, although again for reasons never fully explained. Drink? Nerves? A lack of proper arrangements? Danny Halperin's account of what might have been makes fascinating reading.

'When the tour reached Toronto, I was quite disappointed; my only glimpse of Reinhardt at the concert was when Ellington brought him onstage, introduced him to the audience, and then watched pensively while the guitarist walked into the wings without having played a note.

'After a series of the usual obstacles which dogged anyone who tried to pin down where Ellington could be from one moment to the next, I ended up well after midnight in the home of a French executive of Eaton's, College Street, one of the major Canadian department stores. Besides Ellington, Reinhardt and Kay Davis, who was then singing with the orchestra, and the executive and his family and a few friends, there was with us a member of Ellington's behind-the-scenes organisation whose name I have forgotten. He was a handsome, self-assured man, and he insisted on chatting with me about the novels of Marie Corelli. I had read some of them many years before and could not remember them; he could recall whole passages, which he recited to me while Ellington played his characteristic ripples on the piano.

'Reinhardt pulled up a chair behind him, and Ellington turned to talk to him in what was evidently a sign-language they had developed which consisted of nodding their heads while they smiled happily at each other. The executive's wife asked Miss Davis to sing *April In Paris*. She did not know the lyrics. Someone did, and fed them to her in whispers while she sang and Ellington played.

'Reinhardt took out his guitar and chorded behind her and the piano, and then, without stopping, the guitarist and Ellington segued into *Body And Soul;* Ellington played the first sixteen bars, Reinhardt the release and final eight, and continued for five choruses, each one more haunting and melancholy than the last.

'In the midst of Reinhardt's penultimate chorus, Ellington stopped playing and turned to look at the guitarist, who sat hunched over his instrument, jacket askew, smoke from a cigarette wreathing his smile. At Reinhardt's final chord, he and Ellington sat looking at each other as if they were looking into each other. I said something extravagant and enthusiastic about the way Django had played. Oh well, you know, said the man who had read all of Marie Corelli, they do that *every* night.'

In 1947, back in Paris, and with Grappelli also back in Paris, there was a serious attempt to revive the original Quintet of the Hot Club. And the one positive result was on disc: some of their very best efforts, including *Tiger Rag* (the fastest I've ever heard it played!), *Dinah, Them There Eyes* and reworkings of *Tears, Daphne, Manoir De Mes Rêves* and *Danse Nuptiale*. Stephane's harmonics at the beginning of *Daphne* are something else. There's also a *How High The Moon* (newly become the National Anthem of be-bop) which reveals that the violinist had mastered the new idiom while Django had not. Other than on these sessions though the latter was decidedly unhappy, riddled with neuroses and self-doubt. As Stephane puts it: 'He was disappointed by his failure in New York. He felt everyone was against him.' Added to which a bitter feud had developed between Panassié and Delaunay, the result of their political views, a struggle to control the magazine *Jazz Hot* and Panassié's hatred of modern jazz whereas Delaunay announced he would bring Charlie Parker and other modernists to Europe.

When I heard Django in Paris early in 1951 he was using an amplifier – somewhat clumsily – and had elected to work with a be-bop group he sounded completely out of. Stephane was endeavouring to build a new career for himself, which wasn't easy, but at least it can be said of his playing that he would get better and better. Django's career was like the embers of a gypsy fire. His music was sour; he misused his body. The heart-attack came as no surprise.

Chapter THREE

Jazz is the Esperanto of music. You can go anywhere in the world and play it with good musicians without needing to rehearse. Art Tatum was the equivalent of Horowitz; but he didn't usually rehearse. I don't unless it's something new.

–S. GRAPPELLI, 1974

THE WAR YEARS were unkind to Stephane as well. By the end there was no problem in England about finding good musicians to work with – George Shearing, Alan Clare, Jack Parnell. But there was still a problem in making a living – certainly after being used to higher earnings and some degree of affluence in France. Stephane might have gained the admiration of other jazzmen, but without Django he had nothing like the drawing power he does today. Also, there were the wartime restrictions. Concerts, except for the troops, became rare events. There was broadcasting admittedly; but unless you were George Formby or Tommy Handley the BBC didn't pay very much. Mainly, therefore, it was playing in restaurants and taking what they offered. The government was strict about what could be charged for a meal: five shillings a head at the most. As a result, owners of the smarter West End establishments could only keep going if they charged a fancy price for their dwindling supplies of French and other European wines. There wasn't a lot left over to pay the musicians.

So, Stephane was cut off from his homeland, for all he knew his apartment was being occupied by some Nazi officer, either looting or smashing his embryo collection of antiques and other *objets d'art;* and it came back to scratching for a weekly wage. The man is a great survivor. Of this there can be no doubt. But in spirit he had never felt so low. Because in addition he was dangerously, and in his own mind at one stage, terminally ill.

Doctor (Jack) Harrisson and his wife Audrey are the most longstanding of the violinist's friends in England. 'I first met Steph

In the World War II film, 'Time Flies'.

at Hatchett's Restaurant,' the doctor told me. 'He was working there as the leader of a group that also had George Shearing on piano. His health had been bad, almost touch and go in fact. A doctor doesn't divulge details of the cause – but it was very serious. Anyway, fortunately the treatment – by my father – was successful, and since my father was also the Earl of Sandwich's doctor he arranged for Stephane to convalesce at Hinchinbrooke Castle. I was a big fan of course. And so I was delighted when he came back down to live near us in Devon. [The Harrissons are still at The Yellow Cottage, Bovey Tracey.] That would have been in 1941 – and on account of the war property was fairly cheap. Steph bought a house called Underwood at Lustleigh and I met up with him nearly every week. He'd completely recovered by this time, but it left him very conscious of good health and the need to take care of it. At first he even talked of growing his own vegetables, but that would have been difficult because his garden had a forty-five degree angle slope! All told he lived at Underwood for five years, and even today,

Stephane at a broadcast in 1943.

whenever he plays a concert in the West of England, say at Exeter, he'll break his journey to visit us. Often playing a little impromptu jazz while Audrey is getting the tea or serving drinks.

'During the war years Steph did quite a lot of broadcasts, but because of the air-raids over London it meant him travelling up to Bangor. He worked with the organist Robin Richmond there. Then at the end of the war he went back to the West End and played cabaret and for dancing again.'

The violinist also speaks of touring during the war. 'Let me see. It must have been 1942 or '43. We toured Scotland. Everybody was in the army so I had a hard time forming a band in London specially for the tour. I had George Shearing on piano. George would be about nineteen or twenty and I'd first heard him in a Battersea pub playing accordion. And my drummer Dave Fullerton was from Dundee. We had Beryl Davis and Gloria Brent as our vocalists and we took along some girls to amuse the troops. I remember we stopped in Dundee for a week and every day I took George on my arm into a cinema there to see a film called *Reveille For Beverley*. We'd go in just for five minutes to hear Frank Sinatra sing *Night And Day*. The cinema staff thought we were crazy. But Sinatra sang the song so well.'

When Stephane did return to London he found it a curious mixture of euphoria at the war's being over and austerity under the chancellorship of Sir Stafford Cripps. Evelyn Waugh's Arthur Box-Bender and many more only slightly less fictional Conservative MPs had lost their parliamentary seats to Labour in the general election of 1945. There had been a very difficult winter, with coal shortages, the helping hand of US President Harry S. Truman, his Secretary of State Dean Acheson and the Marshall Plan and not much money to spare for going out at night. Box-Bender was fairly typical of the old smart set and he now had to share a debutante's dance for his eighteen-year-old daughter. The men wore hired evening-dress and Box-Bender and his fellow-host had been at pains to find the cheapest fizzy wine on the market. Again there wasn't a lot left over to pay the musicians. George Shearing already had the idea of making a fresh start in America. Other British players would follow him. (Shearing's reunion with Grappelli would have to wait until the 1970s and an LP with Andrew Simpkins on bass and Rufus Jones on drums. *I'm Coming Virginia, La Chanson De Rue, Star Eyes* et al.)

One musician who did work with Stephane in this immediate post-war period though was Jack Parnell, at the time just beginning to establish himself as the country's leading drummer and who would go on to power-drive Ted Heath's music before leading his own big band. I asked him about those days with Steph.

'Well,' he began, 'we mostly played polite jazz to the accompaniment of knives and forks. We had George Shearing with us for a bit, Dave Goldberg on guitar, Charlie Short, bass, me on the drums. It was my first really important job. I mean to play with Stephane was a great honour. Okay, so people still tended to underrate him, but he had the touch of genius, a French kind of clear, straightforward violin style allied with jazz. The man was a terrific influence, a consummate musician and he's been the same right from the beginning. He's always Stephane, always himself, always well-dressed – and one felt good just being in his presence. Most of all for Dave Goldberg, I think, because there he'd be, playing alongside the violin and feeling he'd stepped right into the shoes of Django.

'Steph shaped the whole musical policy of the group. By this time he'd become very much a leader, whereas before, with Django, it had been a case of co-leadership. He was meticulous about keeping up appearances. Especially over the business of drinking. There'd be the briefcase, the famous black briefcase and inside, under his music, the half-bottle of Scotch. But before he went on he'd only ever take one drink. Just enough to settle his nerves. One had to admire him for this. He never seemed to get hooked on the stuff. He'd have the one tot and then the playing would be something tremendous. He had an immense academic background which he used within the jazz. The music came out quite naturally.

'As a man, Steph the person, I'd say you'd have to call him a loner. You never knew what was going on with him. He'd appear in the right place at the right time, correctly dressed for the occasion, smiling, violin under his arm. Then you'd play, it would be very satisfying for everyone, he'd clean the violin, walk off, still smiling, and you wouldn't see him again until the next day. Yes, he definitely was privately private! Never mind. Over the years he's helped his instrument into a kind of popularity it hadn't known before. Although, I do think with jazz the instrument is really only a vehicle for the man's expression. Stephane is a jazzman, he's got the feeling in him. So he happens to play the violin. It could easily have been the tenor-saxophone. Anything he heard and liked he could fit in with. But he took care to surround himself with the right players, the ones who went with his own style. He's patient, but not with inefficiency. Steph is exactly himself, nothing less: very aware of his own position at any given moment in time and able to get his musical artistry out in any situation.'

I asked Jack if he'd agree that Stephane had actually got better over the years; almost in a refined, Asiatic sense, like a mandarin. Was it due to extra concentration or simply pacing himself the more? His reply was unusual but intriguing.

'No! That, my friend, is *ego*. And all good jazzmen have to have it. Steph makes his ego work for him. He's a great player, he believes in himself, he knows what he can do and he does it. The ego carries him through the realms of technical degeneracy so that he doesn't even need to bother about them. He has tremendous technique on the violin, but he's also a jazzman and he can *scheme* his way into exploiting this. Steph's so individual. That's why he can fit in with so many different players. He doesn't have to challenge them. *They* have to come up to *his* standards – which are very, very high. . .

'Obviously with Django things were different. Django never conformed. I remember Steph telling me they got heavily booked in Paris to play for the President of France at the Elysée Palace. Django was still asleep in his caravan. They had to get him up, even give him a wash. Steph went through all those kind of scenes with him. He just took over – because he never lost faith in his own artistry. Also, the two of them jelled. And what a wonderful coalition! As jazzmen each aroused the other's curiosity. The result was marvellous, magical.'

The end of the Parnell playing-association with Grappelli had an almost Gilbert and Sullivanish air about it. Stephane was desperate to find better-paid work – and thought he'd landed the cabaret spot at The Savoy (the hotel, not the theatre). But first he had to audition. The other members of the group were called there for twelve noon. 'I was rooming with Dave Goldberg in those days,' is how Jack tells it, 'and we overslept. By the time we finally made it to The Savoy it was two-thirty and everyone had gone home. Needless to say, Steph hadn't got the job. However, and with the arrogance of youth, I then 'phoned him, apologised for being *a bit* late but said we ought to be paid for going anyway!' For once even the articulate Grappelli was lost for words. The 'phone went down with a chilling crash.

Following the departure of George Shearing, and then after Jack Parnell's going, the musician who became of the utmost importance to Stephane both as a player and a friend was without doubt the keyboard artist Alan Clare. Probably even today it can still be argued that there is no British jazzman Steph rates more highly – and certainly Alan would come to play a vital role in the long overdue and final appreciation of Grappelli which began at the end of the 'sixties, since when just about every year of his renaissance has been its own *annus mirabilis*.

Clare, a Londoner like Shearing, actually began to play piano from the age of three; with wooden blocks tied to the instrument's pedals so his feet could reach them. Also like Shearing he experimented for a time with the piano-accordion. He is regarded as very much a musician's musician: delicate, subtle, with an incredible ear and a knowledge of tunes and pianos which is quite remarkable. His melodic sense is so developed that at times one has to think of him in a similar mould to the great Bill Evans. More importantly from Grappelli's point of view though, he is probably the best accompanying pianist in the country; sensitive, noticeably unselfish and intuitive about another soloist's needs to a point which is almost uncanny. Stephane became so satisfied with Alan's accompaniments that he even went out of his way to help the pianist find a decent place to live, very difficult in those days. There was much bomb-damage, rationing and the latchkey to a flat could cost a small fortune. Nevertheless, resourceful as ever, the violinist got hold of one at Holland Park – where Alan and his wife Bloom still live.

More money was beginning to circulate now. There was a thriving black market (the age of the 'spivs' and 'drones'); and for anyone lucky enough to be in funds a whole new nightlife began to open up. At the same time too the Cripps austerity programme was being matched by an unprecedented government spending spree in other directions. No one growing up then could fail to be in stitches at the non-productive extravagance of the groundnuts scheme in East Africa, the import of an inedible fish called *snoek* from South Africa and most incredible of all, the Gambia egg-farms which cost us twenty pounds for each egg produced. Nor on the home-front at the free wigs, spectacles and the sets of even-rowed false teeth which became known as 'the National Health smile'. The BBC's current comedians had never known such a time. However, Alan Clare remembers that Stephane began to exude a fresh optimism. He was being nagged by some recurring (kidney) pains, but otherwise he felt life itself had taken an upswing. It was hilarious, maybe, but somehow better.

The Grand Reunion with George Shearing.

I asked the pianist how he first became involved with Stephane; together with several other questions: what working with him was like, what were his methods, mannerisms and so on. 'I first met him, briefly, back in 1941,' he told me. 'But then I had to go in the army, so we couldn't play regularly together until the end of the war. George Shearing I'd known since 1940. I'd been introduced to him by Carlo Krahmer who had the band at a place called 'The Boogie-Woogie' in Denman Street. There was an instant rapport between us – I was nearly always over at George's place . . . and so we naturally picked this up once the war ended. We played four-handed duets together and sometimes duets on our piano-accordions.

'When Stephane had the job at Hatchett's he lived just along Piccadilly from there at the Atheneum Hotel, would you believe it paying a rent of three pounds ten shillings a week! And they let him keep a Knight piano in his room. After the war though he had his own pad, a good, big flat at Troy Court in Kensington. Anyway, by this time I had a job at the place in Regent Street which eventually became the Edmundo Ros Club. I played with Frank Weir – and George Shearing and I would often swap gigs. I also used to go rowing with him –'

At this point I felt compelled to interrupt. 'George Shearing, rowing? You're having me on, surely!'

'No, no, we went rowing together. And sometimes I'd challenge him about whether a certain object on the bank was a tree or a lamp-post, and he always knew, even though we were on the water. He told me he could *hear* it as a shadow falling on that side of his head in a certain shape. The thing about George, who as you know was born blind, is that he's extraordinarily developed in every other way, sensitised totally. I can remember once driving him from Hatchett's to up beyond Holborn. This was during the blitz, bombs falling and big bangs everywhere, and George remained completely calm, giving me all the turns and street directions. The only thing he hated was snow. Because it interrupted his hearing, muffling the sounds he knew. If it snowed, and I had to take him back down to his home at Battersea, I literally had to drag him to the car.

'However, I digress. It was as a result of George and I swapping gigs, keeping in touch with the music in other clubs and so on that I came to Stephane's notice as a musician. He began to ask for me and eventually it became a proper job. Until he decided to go back to France. After this there was the long gap before he started to come back to Britain in the 1960s – which sparked off his present world fame. Working with him was, and always will be a great privilege, of course. Even if you have a tiff with him about something there's no denying the quality of musicianship. It's always the same, wonderful. . .

'You asked me about Stephane the man though. Well, really I suppose his character is so multi-dimensional that it's difficult to describe or define in mere words. But he's always logical, always true to himself – and there are lots of little things, stories I could tell you, which tend to fit in with what we know about his music. For instance, he can be kind, charming – but at the same time utterly ruthless in order to get everything right. Because he's so fastidious. He can be as flamboyant about his dress as his music sounds – but this has been designed for its particular effect as well as to satisfy his own tastes. It was just the same with his flat. We'd go around to Troy Court and everything on his desk would be in place, meticulous. All the antiques laid out to their best advantage.'

BLOOM CLARE: 'Also, then he'd come back to *our* place and the first thing he'd do was go around the room straightening all the pictures!'

'Yes, his accuracy is fantastic,' Alan agrees. 'He's so accurate he can kill a fly on the wall with his violin-bow. Although this prompts me to add that his humour is equally fantastic. Mentioning the violin-bow reminds me how he loved to use it to tap the bottoms of ladies dancing past the stand. Then he'd pretend it was all a mistake made while he was raising it to play again! The humour is very quick. He's never lost for a verbal rejoinder. Once, much later, we were going to a broadcast. We had an expensive hire-car and there wasn't much time so we parked it up on the kerb outside a block of flats. Almost immediately an open window was pushed up further and two huge tattooed forearms were planted on the sill. The man (whose face we couldn't see) had obviously mistaken Stephane's French accent as we got out of the car. "Go on, yer damn Jew," he shouted, "bugger off from there!" "Actually," Steph called back, "it so 'appens I am a Catholic. But I don't mind if you call me a damn Jew. I probably have more money than you do anyway!"

'It would be difficult to get the better of him, at least mentally. Which applies very much to this business with the antiques. He doesn't just *acquire* antiques, he also deals in them part of the time.

41

And if you go down the Portobello Road with him he never makes mistakes. He *knows* about them, he has that kind of retentive brain.

'Another time, again much later, we were working at the Les Ambassadeurs Club in Park Lane. We were allowed to have a meal as part of the job but they insisted on keeping us to a break of only fifteen minutes. Not to be outdone, every night Steph managed to get through soup, half a chicken, salad, dessert, wine and coffee in those fifteen minutes – all the while glaring defiance at the manager who was eating his own supper in more leisurely fashion on the other side of the room. There was no giving way. He taught me all the tricks of the trade about working in restaurants.'

'He always appears so on top of things,' I said. 'How about the nerves though, didn't they show through sometimes?'

'Yes. There was always the small Scotch before a performance. But also he would sit there and *rock*. Just gently rocking back and forth on the edge of a chair or a settee. "You can't be an artist unless you have nerves," he once told me. Again, he's quite nervous about personal relationships, certainly to begin with – as I was to find out later when I started booking his musicians for him. He's never afraid of speaking his mind, but he is afraid of ill-health and I think of any physical squaring up – unless he's sure of coming out the winner. Since all that kidney trouble he's taken the utmost care of himself, and the only occasion I saw him indulge in any real violence was the reason why we got the chop at 96 Piccadilly. In fact at that time we were doing two jobs. 96 Piccadilly and the Milroy Club. 96 Piccadilly was essentially a restaurant, the Milroy was a nightclub and we used to go from one to the other. We had Don Fraser on guitar, Russ Allen, bass, and Johnny Flanagan on drums. They were fun times too. I remember one customer asking if we could do *La Veal En Rose*. "No," Stephane quipped. "But we do 'ave the 'Am-On-Eggs!" He could keep us in fits like that.

'The only trouble was the manager at 96, Frank Shaw I think his name was. A real pain. Stephane put it more strongly than that: a real pig, he said. You know, we used to have a lot of celebrities drop in. Jean Sablon, Douglas Byng. But Steph's particular friends among the clientele were Vasco, the painter, and Baron the photographer. Okay, so they were a bit on the wild side. They'd come tearing into the place, slide the length of the dance-floor as if at an ice-rink and crash into the bandstand. But they were good customers and they did spend a lot of money. Anyway, the manager

42

Jean Sablon.

(Photo from 'Jazz Away From Home')

kept on about them, not to their faces, but to Steph as if anything they did was his personal fault. Until one night he finally blew his top. There was a real shout-up, Steph called him a lot of names and it ended with Steph ripping the inside 'phone off the wall. Of course it meant instant dismissal – and I think it was this as much as anything which decided him to go back and try his luck in France.'

One final point I put to him about this particular period in the violinist's life. Had the music now veered away entirely from that of the Quintet of the Hot Club?

'No, not entirely – because of Stephane's own playing and style of swing. But it had certainly changed. Since he was now very much the leader and principal soloist he was able to be more free, more adventurous, more daring with the things he brought out. Perhaps more classical too: the tone and phrasing and those marvellous cadenzas. Again, we were getting so many fresh compositions in from the States. Tremendous tunes out of the new musicals, "Kiss Me Kate" and so on. Songs like *So In Love*. We'd play these every night and it allowed Steph to get away from the old standard repertoire of the Quintet.'

Chapter FOUR

Ennui is the condition of not fulfilling our potentialities; remorse of not having fulfilled them; anxiety of not being able to fulfil them, – but what are they?

THE VIOLIN-MAESTRO was now to enter the last but also the longest period of unhappiness and dissatisfaction with his musical career. Ironically, it was the period when he consolidated his life financially, moving his growing possessions from London to Paris, gaining the apartment at Cannes and his other house near Chartres. Money has always been of tremendous importance to Stephane. Not as a sum in the bank. Not even to buy his clothes and antiques, but as a form of independence. He is haunted by the memories of having once had to play on the streets, not even sure of the price of coffee and bread. 'When once you've starved, you never forget what it is like.' So he went for a regular job and it nearly finished him.

As time went on he would come to be admired by many greats of the jazz world – Duke Ellington, John Lewis (director of the Modern Jazz Quartet) and fellow-violinist Stuff Smith. He would witness the original recordings of the Quintet of the Hot Club used by Louis Malle for the soundtrack of the film *Lacombe, Lucien* and be booked to do TV, to tour the world and play the big festivals at Newport, Nice and Montreux. But through the 1950s and well into the '60s he remained largely forgotten.

The recovery of France after the war was necessarily slower but then steadier than Britain's. The occupation had left her without most things including railways and sugar. Also there was a far-flung empire, first to fight for and then, gradually, to dismantle. Meanwhile the Americans were putting their major effort financially into the refurbishing of Germany. However, French nationalism and logicality soon reasserted themselves. Left free, the country can always feed itself – and consequently what industrial products can be exported represent a profit. This fact, plus a pragmatic attitude within the European Community, has given modern France (since the 1950s) a degree of affluence which has eluded several of her neighbours. Stephane would share in this affluence, but the sacrifice of much pride and integrity was almost too much to bear. For year after year he languished at the Paris Hilton (the *Le Toit* club), on a very good salary but by and large unappreciated by a clientele (rich American tourists, French *parvenus*) who knew little about jazz and cared considerably less. His name meant nothing to them; he was there as background. Often he'd be told to play quieter while they got on with their talk over the drinks.

Reluctant to give up the security, he gritted his teeth and banked the cheques. There were no new recordings and so the jazz world came to regard him as a spent force. Which reinforced the argument for Django being called the only real star of the old Quintet of the

1961. On the B.B.C. TV show, 'Soft Lights And Sweet Music'.

Hot Club. When the guitarist died suddenly in 1953 there was a mad scramble to collect every record he'd ever played on, even rough air-shots. Stephane was the also-ran. Eventually, feeling thoroughly miserable, he paid a short visit to London and poured out his frustrations to Alan Clare – who told him quite bluntly to quit the Hilton and start travelling his art again. Alan was satisfied the violinist was playing better than ever; he just had to make the decision. And fortunately this time he did.

London was as good a launching pad as any. After that they were ready to take on the world. So that when Stephane next returned to Britain he was an international star. It meant he could pull in the crowd at Ronnie Scott's and even at the Albert Hall (with a concert celebrating his 70th birthday). There would be a Royal Command Performance and, surprise, surprise, the dubious accolade of a *This Is Your Life!* Since when Stephane has even elected to have a British manager.

Edward 'Ed' Baxter was running the box-office at the Usher Hall in Edinburgh when they first met. Originally a lover of classical

Accompanying Carole Carr.

music, he was urged by John Gibson of *The Evening News* to book a jazz artist for the Edinburgh Festival and chose Grappelli. 'The only jazz player I knew at the time!' Stephane packed the theatre every night which amazed everyone concerned (it wouldn't today). Also, as Ed explains, 'he liked the way it was all going and asked me to arrange his other tours. Steph had been through a lot of trouble with his business arrangements. But we trusted each other instantly.' Now, whenever Grappelli tours Britain, Ed leaves his box-office in the charge of his wife and daughter and travels with him. 'He's really become a part of the family. We've got used to his nerves before a concert. He always has ten minutes or so when he is very quiet and emotional.'

Ed also confirms what Grappelli has said about avoiding rehearsals – you just go in there and play. 'Steph never likes to know what the arrangements are beforehand,' and he cited an appearance he was due to make at the Festival Hall with the brillant young 'cellist Julian Lloyd Webber. 'No programme has been arranged yet. We just know that they will turn up and play some tunes. That's about all.'

I went back to the Clares to learn more about the start of the Grappelli revival. As well as to flesh out this portrait of Stephane by recording on cassette from Alan's long-term memory.

'Did you know he took some lessons with Alfredo Campoli during the war?' he asked me sharply.

'No –' (Another strange twist – because what I did know was that Campoli, the famous classical violinist, had himself been 'depping' during the war for the called-up Oscar Grasso with Victor Silvester's band.)

'Well, he did. But for some reason I've never been able to understand, he always seems to want to hide the fact that he's so well-trained. I believe he won a prize at the Paris Conservatoire. I asked Yehudi Menuhin once if Steph's approach to the violin was academic, formal, and he said yes, quite definitely. Also you can't play all those things he does on the piano without being properly taught. Fauré, Debussy, Ravel. He can play them from memory. He was influenced by the whole French tradition in music – and then by jazz. He's a Bach fanatic too. In fact it's his usual practice-piece, to do some Bach. He enjoys all music to play, but he doesn't like to have it played to him any more. He wouldn't listen to the car-radio when we went on tour. He was more interested in looking at the countryside or stopping and visiting old churches. Well, he's spent so much time in Britain now – and he's really become very knowledgeable about it. Perhaps it has a lot to do with this later, much more successful part of his career actually starting here.'

BLOOM CLARE: 'Going back to those Campoli lessons though. They nearly killed him jazzwise, he said. "That man almost ruined my wrists," he said. "He was good, but he would have spoiled my natural way of swinging." He'd had all the formal training as a young man, but his jazz methods were entirely his own.' She served the tea and cakes. 'Again, he went on at me regularly for not singing more. I had a family to look after, I said. But he either couldn't or wouldn't accept my not trying to make money as a singer. He said it was like throwing diamonds in the dustbin. . .'

ALAN: 'We never met his wife. In fact for a while I thought she must have died, then we heard she was living in the South of France. Evelyn, his daughter, we do know of course – she's married to a restaurant-owner, also in the South. Then there's the grandson, young Steph – a chip off the old block if ever you saw one. He usually makes a beeline for us when he's in town. There's a second grandson I believe, but I haven't met him.

'But you asked me about when things started up again in the 1960s. Well, I can tell you without any exaggeration it was often hilarious, pure pantomime. Not so much getting the work. That built up gradually. The more he played the more the public heard how good he was as a soloist, and so we started to get the lot then, concerts, broadcasts, TV from Ronnie Scott's, the Edinburgh Festival and finally of course the Parkinson Show, when suddenly he found himself accepted and admired by whole millions. But all the business I went through with other players for the group, *that was hilarious.*

'Or so it seems now. At the time it was a constant headache. Steph is as excessively fastidious about the choice of accompanying players as he is about his clothes, antiques and so on. In his case the style of jazz is equally true to the man. In fact, the only player I've ever known get away with (a few) things apropos Stephane has been Disley. However he gets plenty of Steph's verbals as well – that much I do know. Also, you can't do anything with Diz. He just puts his own chaos together and it's like it's happening straight off the cuff. He's another gypsy, another little Django. In fairness too

(Photo David Redfern)

The new resurgence.

he does have his other uses in the group – although a couple of times I've had to ask myself what exactly they are!

'I'm digressing again though. While Steph was exacting about the standards of musicianship, my job in booking the men would be complicated and sometimes rendered nearly impossible by his suddenly getting a thing about one of them. It was purely physical – some factor that made him go off the guy. And it nearly always revolved about the *heyes!* That and the drummers.'

I should explain at this point what Alan means by 'heyes'. Stephane has come to speak – and to write as well – pretty good English. Although as Len Skeat told me, if the occasion to *his* mind requires otherwise he will do a De Gaulle and pretend not to understand. 'If someone wants to drag him to a party and he doesn't want to go. Or when people turn up at the stage-door with old violins to sell or wanting a free valuation. Then he'll duck out by insisting he doesn't know the lingo. But he's never lost for words when he's after something!'

On the other hand, the violinist does have the normal French problem with our 'th' sound. 'Tonight I play for you *Teese Foolish Tings*,' he will say. And likewise he drops a lot of his aitches and then puts this same consonant in where it oughtn't to be. Hence 'heyes' for 'eyes'.

'Yes, it was *heyes* and the drummers that used to spark things off,' Alan continues. 'First of all I got Tony Crombie on drums. Afterwards Steph said he was an excellent player – but there was something about the *heyes* which unnerved him. They were too dark, yes black, like a gangster's. I argued with him that in fact Tony is as sweet as a nut – a very gentle guy. But Steph wouldn't have it. "No, 'e frightens me," he insisted. "As 'e played the batterie, 'e looked at me a bit funny, as if 'e want to attack me or something!" So I had to tell Tony, it's no good, you scare him. And he said, with typical Jewish fatalism: "Lovely. I don't get the bleedin' job on account of the colour of my eyes. I've never had that no-no before!" So next I got Bobby Orr – who played an absolute storm. But Bobby's a typical Highlander, who that day had had a terrible row with someone, I believe to do with his car. Anyway he came in with those bright eyes of his all ablaze – so again Stephane goes on at me about the *heyes*. "Who is tis one?" he asked me. And I told him it was Bobby Orr. "Oh," he said. "Well, look, 'e got tat wild blue heye. Tat kind of Scottish heye. I tell you, tat strange look 'e 'as definitely makes me feel nervous. I bet 'e got tat bloody big sword stuck down 'is sock. 'E might try to kill me, tis one!" So Bobby, another sweet guy, had to go. Really all because he'd had a row with someone else over a damn car.

'Then we had Chris Karan, which was fine – except that he had a very bad stomach ulcer which he had to feed regularly – and at one session Steph noticed him every so often glancing at his watch. So it all began again. "Tis one, 'e don't care about the music. First we 'ave the black heyes, ten the wild blue heye and now tis one who always 'as 'is heyes on the time." Chris tried to be helpful by pointing out that if the session went overtime it would cost more money. But Stephane was not to be placated. "Ah, man, we got another of tose," he said. And he called over to Chris, "Maybe your watch is too fast, Monsieur!"

'Well, after *all* of this palaver, we were playing at Ronnie Scott's (with Chris) – and Tony Crombie was on drums with the other group, playing very well but also in a marvellous mood, laughing and joking between the numbers. Suddenly Steph's leaning over towards me and saying, "Surely tis is the one we should get. Look, 'es so jolly!" I blew my top! I said, what are you talking about? This is the one with the black eyes. The one you wouldn't let me hire at any price. Now you've really dropped me in the shit. Because when I go over there and ask him to play with us, he'll think it was *me*, not *you* who didn't want him in the first place!

'However, as luck would have it Stephane got his come-uppance just a few minutes later – and Britain's drummers their own back. For as we walked out of Ronnie's who should be there, as if waiting for us, but the late Phil Seaman – of all drummers the absolute master of the *heyes*. He was sick and gone, away up there on Mars almost, but he grabbed hold of Stephane's arm and he was very strong, just like the Ancient Mariner. He peered at him from under those bushy blonde eyebrows he had, and then he said: "Listen, mate, one of these nights I'm going to come up there and stick some rhythm right up your arse. And when I do you're going to fuckin' wonder what's happened!" Stephane was petrified, I've never seen him so shaken. All he could do was murmur, "Yes, of course, tank

A little gentler, please!

(*Photo David Redfern*)

(*Photo courtesy B.B.C.*)

Music is serious, of course. . . .

you, tank you, Monsieur". Then to me, after Phil let go his arm, he said, out of the corner of his mouth: "And who is tis one?" I told him. "Man," he said, "tis is the most frightening heye of all, the heye of the drugger. C'mon, let's go before 'e catch 'old of me again." I never saw him walk so fast.'

After this incident Alan was left alone to recruit the musicians. The violinist had been taught to trust him. As for Lennie Bush, the group's outstanding bass-player, evidently he had the mild and friendly, not the wicked *heyes*. (Meanwhile, for the convenience of the reader, from now on and in most places I will attribute the normal 'th' and 'h' sounds to Stephane.)

Meanwhile too the so-called Swinging Sixties in Britain were turning into the decayed and uncertain '70s. Harold Macmillan's 'You've Never Had It So Good' slogan (which won the Tories their election and persuaded half the work force that it didn't really need to work) had been followed by Harold Wilson's so-called 'White Hot Technological Revolution' and then further financial disasters. Edward Heath's brave start in 1970 was overturned by the miners' strike and after this the road to recession lay open. Strangely enough though, this did not at first affect the world of entertainment. It was almost as if people were prepared to make sacrifices in other directions rather than forego their short breaks of escape. And Stephane, an unassailable celebrity now, simply couldn't miss. Every club date was packed, every concert sold out. Back in his native France too he was at last accepted as the country's outstanding jazz musician. No wonder the photographs of his being presented to Queen Elizabeth II after the Royal Variety Show of 1972 show him looking extremely contented with life. To borrow a couplet from John Dryden: 'The Prince long time had courted Fortune's love/But once possessed did absolutely reign. . .'

But still a thing to enjoy.

(Photo courtesy B.B.C.)

The next change in his music occurred at the end of 1973 when Alan Clare decided to quit touring. 'I felt like I'd been at it for a hundred years, and now it was me who wanted a residency somewhere. Steph begged me not to go, but this time I had to refuse him.'

They had done the Edinburgh Festival; their last important engagement was at the Chichester Festival Theatre in September, 1973 – again with Lennie Bush on bass and the black-*heyed* Tony Crombie on drums. There was an emotional farewell party after the show and Stephane decided that he wouldn't look for another piano-player – except for special occasions like a recording session. As regards the future public work he would try to start up something new.

By now though I too had become like Coleridge's buttonholing Mariner, not yet ready to let the subject go. I asked Alan about their actual working methods over the crucial years of the musical partnership. And I asked both Bloom and Alan if they could put into ordinary human terms what their longstanding friendship has been like with the violinist.

'Our working methods,' the pianist stressed, 'go right back to those early days at 96 Piccadilly and the Milroy Club. The only big difference that took place over the years was the change from playing for dancers and diners to giving concerts and recitals. I personally preferred the former, although we didn't let the more 'stagey' work of more recent years interfere with our *basic* rapport. We just had to give it a more extrovert face. Which Steph, of course, revels in!' (It's interesting to add here that Count Basie once told me he thought jazz had changed for the worse when the bands couldn't play for dancing any longer.)

'At 96 Piccadilly especially we would set about each new number direct from the sheet-copy. And since we were in a resident job, by developing it in action we could test out our arrangement as we went along, building it into a satisfactory shape and form. Then we'd gradually refine and improve it until the overall piece was good for all seasons – with just the solos improvised, but their length predetermined. There'd be people up on the dance-floor for everything we played, and Stephane's own playing was particularly great just then. We used to get the customers, clientele, call them what you like, kind of mesmerised with what we did. They used to fall in love and get married because of the way we played. Yes, truly! We'd get them into this semi-swooning state – and then the next week they'd come back and tell us they had just been married, and it'd happened as a result of the magical atmosphere we'd created from the bandstand. We would watch them going around the floor in a dream almost. And when the number ended, they didn't want to believe it. They'd go back to their tables, but very slowly, as if reluctant to lose their hold on the dream.

'For us, this kind of audience response was really tremendous. Inspiring. And in time each individual number became like a kind of moulded theatre piece, a short play in three acts: the theme, the solos and the recapitulation. Moulded together until it was well-nigh perfect. We'd have created our own special introduction and coda to each tune, so we didn't need to say, Oh number ninety-two next. I've had all that in other places: twelve, twenty-eight, sixty – just numbers in the bandbook. Horrible! With Steph, he'd play the intro and I knew which piece it was immediately. I looked forward to every single tune he picked.

'Often as well we'd work out some very complicated harmonies. Chord sequences which many years later have left even a great bass-player like Lennie (Bush) almost pole-axed with surprise and admiration. But we always made them fit with the melody-line and the tempo. Again these too would be developed on the bandstand. We'd swap ideas and they'd come out right because we were plugged in to each other's thinking and style. Don Fraser, the guitarist, was in on this alongside us. Actually, Don was a very underrated player – and incidentally the first guitarist I ever heard make use of a foot-pedal to vary his sound. In the solos Steph used to like me to fly around the keyboard, featuring plenty of technique. And at the Milroy Club the other band was Santiago's, a genuine Brazilian unit – which I'd often sit in with and thoroughly enjoyed. But that wasn't really Steph's bag, Latin-American music. Nor was he a great jam session man. He obviously prefers his own formal setting.

'Another thing I noticed is that he's almost equally formal about how he spends his day. He doesn't like to get up much before twelve – even though he's probably been awake for hours. Then he might go shopping or visit some place of interest – but making sure there'll be no last minute rush back if he has to play that evening. He has to have his bath and appear at the performance in immaculate attire. Always. He's also a very determined walker –

(*Photo Tim Motion*)

With Marian Montgomery.

which constitutes a further part of his life style. After our finish at the Milroy Club, at two and sometimes three in the morning, and provided the weather wasn't too bad, he'd then walk the length of Piccadilly and on to Troy Court, by Kensington High Street. Even today he's forever walking, walking, walking. Which I think is the main reason why he's so fit. And make no mistake about it, he's *very* fit, just like wire. That's his secret formula: good, regular sleep and a lot of walking.'

BLOOM CLARE: 'The last time he came here to dinner he walked all the way from the Edgware Road, from Park West. But he said that, knowing I'm a *cordon bleu* cook he wanted to make certain of reaching us with a sufficient appetite. Talk about charm! Because as you probably know he's a fantastic eater. Quantity as well as quality. And I definitely have his approval as a cook. Which means like the feeding of the five thousand – only with something more than just loaves and fishes!

'On one occasion though he turned up and asked me if I'd make

With John Ogden.

him a sandwich. Because he had a snack. Which struck me as being
a bit peculiar – even given Steph's capacity. He wanted a sandwich
but he'd just eaten a snack? I said, I can make you a sandwich or I
can do you a snack. "No, no," he said, "I need a sandwich because
I 'ave a snack." By this time I was thoroughly confused, so I just
went out and made him an extra-large sandwich. Only after he'd
polished it off – in double-quick time – did the truth come out.
When he said *snack* what he really meant was *snake*, yes, he had a
tapeworm! He'd eaten some bad pork and was going to hospital the
next day to have treatment for it.

'Anyway, that night we went along to hear Alan play at the Star
Club in Wardour Street (nicknamed the Scar Club because of all the
villains who drank there) – and after about an hour Al began to play
his own composition *Mirage,* which as you know has a distinctively
oriental, Middle Eastern sound to it. Especially when another
musician called Frank Freeman joined in on flute. I suggested to
Steph therefore that if Alan played the tune for long enough, then

he wouldn't need to go into the hospital. The music would charm the snake right up through his mouth! Well, in all the time I've known him, I've never seen Steph laugh so much. He was in hysterics, bent over double at what I'd said.

'Actually he not only loves jokes, he's very good at picking up the subtler ones you wouldn't think he'd understand – but most of all, and being typically French, he loves jokes about *merde*. Also he likes to use English swear-words. Okay, so he's a very sophisticated guy – but even after all these years our traditional Anglo-Saxon swear-words still sound novel, *and emphatic*, to him.

'When his daughter Evelyn was over with him, she was only about fourteen at the time, and she spoke no English – so I used to take her out shopping and so on, doing the best I could with my original schoolgirl French. Well, it was Christmas-time and she wanted to buy her father a dressing-gown as a present – so I took her up to my uncle's place, where you could get them at cost. Anyway, I had to speak to her in French – and that again gave Steph pleasure, hearing my mistakes in the language. Because, you know,

With Lena Martell.

(Photo courtesy B.B.C.)

he's a great mimic – and he'd keep saying to me, "Go on, say that once more, once more, please!" Evelyn was a very sweet girl. And Stephane was often too busy to give her much time, although he could be a strict father. I remember we had to talk him into letting her go with us to a fancy-dress evening – and we helped her make up a costume with the clothes she had, just a beret and jersey and short skirt so she could go as a French *apache*. But she also got back at him by imposing a franc fine every time she caught him swearing. "Ah, Papa, you have used a bad word again!" It's as well she didn't know English then.' Bloom wondered whether she should have instructed Evelyn in our coarser vernacular. 'She would have made a fortune. Five hundred pounds a week at least!'

'Other times Steph would beg me to make "those special little cakes," which were almond macaroons basically – almonds, sugar and egg-whites – of which he was passionately fond. Yes, usually in the end his visits would always bring in something to do with his tummy! But one day we realised just how much he trusted us when he brought round his violin and asked us to look after it for him. He was going off somewhere, I think on a short holiday – or sniffing out antiques. Now Stephane has often quipped that he plays on a piece of wood fitted to a cigar-box, but even in those days – the 1950s – his instrument was worth almost a thousand pounds: an awful lot of money then. I didn't know this to begin with, so of course I said yes. To me it was just another violin and we were doing a friend, well a favour or a gesture of good will. Afterwards, when Alan told me what it was worth, I nearly fainted. After all, the whole of our furniture and everything we had in those days didn't come to a thousand pounds. So we kept it under the bed – and I was afraid to leave the flat until Steph came back and collected it!'

Was the violinist very temperamental to work with?

'Yes, oh he can be,' Alan confirmed. 'If things aren't just right or going his way. But I personally wasn't ever subjected to any of the tantrums, the jumping up and down and so on. In fact, from a purely physical point of view he's always been somewhat cautious with me. Ever since the time I grabbed him by the lapels and actually shook him. I shook him all the way round the bandroom.'

Why?

'Oh, he'd been messing me around. And then he swore at me onstage. For something which was his fault. So when he came off I was waiting for him. And I'm tougher than he is.'

59

BLOOM CLARE: 'The next day, Steph crept round to the flat and tapped on the door, but hesitantly, as if preparing to run. "Is 'e in," he said, "that one?" Yes, but he's asleep, I said. Then he visibly relaxed. "Thank God for that", he said. "Last night he tried to kill me, your 'usband. He's a maniac. Look: he's nearly ripped the lapels off my suit. And my best suit too!" I couldn't resist giggling. Anyway, then Alan got up and immediately they were friends again.'

ALAN: 'The only other set-to we had was when we did cabaret at The Savoy. He said something to me and I answered in kind – adding that I wasn't frightened of him and he'd better watch it. Well, the very next day we had a recording session at Lansdowne House, and when I got there he was sitting on the wall outside. "Man," he said, "I hope you're not going to attack me today. You know, I get frightened of you sometimes. When you've got that stare, yes, the heye! Then I think you are going to kill me." I said, yeah, sometimes I think I am too. Then he started his rocking, you know. "Man," he said, "don't say things like that! I love you like a brother. You are the finest one that I play with all this time. We must not to argue." So then we went in and did the session and it was one of the best sessions we ever played together. But then they're like that, the French. All in a rage, shouting and screaming one moment and seconds later it's been forgotten. British musicians aren't like that. There's less of a row in the first place, maybe nothing even said to the guy's face, but then it's allowed to fester and you can be sure it'll come out later, often quite dangerously.

'Steph's marvellous really. Quick-tempered, yes. But I've never known him bear a grudge.'

Chapter *FIVE*

Meanwhile it is eve. Let us receive every influx of real strength and tenderness. And at dawn, armed with infinite patience, we shall enter splendid cities.

— RIMBAUD, *L'Enfer*

O N FIRST thinking about it the great French poet would seem to have more in common with Django than Grappelli. Wild, a wanderer, no more writing after the age of eighteen, then a trader and even a gun-runner, in Cyprus, in Ethiopia, and dead at thirty-six, following the amputation of one of his legs with an enormous tumour. But there are near-miracles in the difficult teenage genius of his poetry which create their own sounding-boards upon those of us who are prepared to pause and listen to the cry. Stephane did have the strength and patience to last his way through the years of neglect. And now he has entered the splendid cities. There isn't a capital in the world which would not welcome him as a master of his craft.

The 'eve' period was the one with Alan Clare: when his reputation was being re-established and his artistry finally recognised in full. Since 1974 the high tide of life has been wherever he's chosen to go.

Stephane first of all toyed with the idea of having a group, his group, and also having Alan Clare join him as a special guest just to accompany him for the ballads. But the pianist was adamant about no more touring. So, the group came into being as we still know it today. (Premiered at the Cambridge Folk Festival of 1973.) A modified version of the old Hot Club sound, with solo violin, two acoustic guitars and a double bass. Stephane even planned the actual stage layout, with the others in a horseshoe shape around him, the bass in the middle and a guitar on either side. On several occasions billed as the Diz Disley Trio, his first accompanists were Disley and Denny Wright playing the guitars and Len Skeat on bass.

The presentation to H.M. Elizabeth II. In the background Jack Parnell.

Although born in Canada, Disley in most other ways is very much a scion of the Yorkshire where he grew up. He attended the Leeds College of Art and had his cartoons published in *Melody Maker* and other journals before devoting himself to the guitar. His musical background before joining Stephane was mainly skiffle, folk clubs and such 'trad' jazz bands as Mick Mulligan's and Ken Colyer's. But he was a Django admirer and at one point led a quintet of three guitars, violin and bass. Denny Wright's career had been a lot more varied. At the age of eighteen he did in fact play with Stephane at Hatchett's Restaurant when George Shearing was still around. Following which his guitar talents took him out on nearly every branch of the musical tree. He played lead guitar on such 'pop' hits as Lonnie Donegan's *Cumberland Gap* and Johnny Duncan's *Last Train To San Fernando* as well as leading his own Latin-American band. Widely-regarded as an outstanding technician on his instrument, he has the ability to play a very hard-driving rhythm in addition to his fine solos.

Len Skeat became known to Stephane in quite a different way. During the 1973 Edinburgh Festival, in fact. For some reason Lennie Bush couldn't do the gig and so Alan Clare picked Len as a replacement. Stephane was so impressed that he promptly invited Len to join his new group. The bass player had had immense experience, working with Ted Heath, Ronnie Scott, Tubby Hayes, Lou Rawls, The Supremes and more recently he has been playing with Ruby Braff and Eddie 'Lockjaw' Davis. He plays with a big tone and an almost formal sound, which combined with his swing and solo abilities made him an ideal player for Grappelli. He's also proven something like a Virgil to me through the next sections of the book; because for three years, until he too ceased touring, he was the one member of the group Steph nearly always elected to travel with, and his memory of the American, Australian and many other journeyings is as sharp as a razor. He often took a small cartridge recorder along and there are fascinating snatches of Grappelli on location.

Enjoying the organ-practice at Durham Cathedral, for instance. And then in discussion (with obvious knowledge) about architecture and mediaeval churches. He marvels at the size and splendour of Niagara Falls. 'Natural, fabulous. And look at the rainbow! Since the beginning of the earth it's been falling like this. Absolutely incredible!' While in Australia he plays two sets which are as dazzling as anything I've ever heard by him. *Tea For Two*, Django's *Mirage, The Birth Of The Blues*, Michel Legrand's *(What Are You Doing) The Rest Of Your Life?, I Can't Give You Anything But Love, Summertime, Limehouse Blues, Deep River, You Go To My Head* and *It Might As Well Be Spring*. The numbers flow out from

Denny Wright.

Diz Disley.

between bow and finger like musical nectar. Then he does a quick tune-up and it's into *Lady Be Good, I Got Rhythm, After You've Gone, The Nearness Of You, Lover Come Back To Me, Honeysuckle Rose* (with scarcely a reference to the original melody as he races into tempo) and finally *Misty* (a concise, pithy tribute to the late Erroll Garner). At the end one can hear Ronnie Scott, who also played on the tour, break into genuine eulogies. 'Other violinists might be more earthy, more bluesy, but no one plays the standards like this – and with ballads he's in a class all on his own.'

There's a snippet too of Nigel Kennedy, the gifted young English violinist Steph has taken an interest in, playing *Tiger Rag;* and in conclusion another visit to Doctor and Audrey Harrisson. This latter grew into something of a party. There's much chat about the rates going up. Then Disley entertains the company with a rendition of *The Prune Song* while drinks are being served. Ike Isaacs (who had replaced Denny Wright by this date) strums some rhythm and between whisky and sandwiches Steph gets out his fiddle and plays *You Took Advantage Of Me* and *How High The Moon.* Eventually he left bearing soup-plates and a bag of sugar. Into the Devon rain.

'Why sugar though?' I asked.

LEN: 'Oh, he scrounged some wherever we went on that tour. There'd been some official announcement: that there might be a shortage. So Steph said we had to be prepared . . .

'When the new group got under way, Diz Disley was prepared to do more than just play the guitar. Until Ed Baxter came into the picture Diz did most of the legwork. Setting up things and so on – almost like a player-manager. And of course he used to go on stage first and crack a few jokes to get the audience relaxed for when he introduced Stephane.

'We rarely rehearsed. We had a fairly set programme – which we had to remember to vary if we played the same town say, six months later. Steph's actual knowledge of tunes is remarkable, quite remarkable, but he could be very stubborn about not wanting to change the working formula. Maybe we'd add a fresh number, then other times we'd rehearse something new and come the show he'd leave it out. He loved me to play *Satin Doll,* as my bass solo *every night* – until I got thoroughly sick of the piece. And when Denny Wright left he said he'd never play *Sweet Georgia Brown* again as long as he lived. I don't know whether Steph was afraid to change a

(Photo courtesy Len Skeat)

A taste for eye-catching shirts.

Len Skeat (with Bobby Tucker).

(Photo Denis J. Williams)

winning programme, but it was awfully hard to get him to budge. Which kind of imposed restrictions on his great talent.

'In other ways though he can be very quick to make up his mind. The first time I met him, in Edinburgh, with Alan Clare, he listened to me run through a couple of numbers and I was okay, booked. However, he was then extra fussy about my actual appearance. He wanted me to have highly-coloured shirts – and over the next three years I had to keep buying these bright, flashy shirts for the stage-work.

'The test night with the guitar group was at The Bull's Head, in Barnes. Then to get the ball rolling we started doing folk clubs, the sort of places Diz had played before. Which in turn led to the chain of tours, all over the world, getting bigger and better the whole time. The biggest success of all though came after Steph did the Parkinson Show. Grappelli with Menuhin. That was the key to it. It seemed like *everybody* had watched the show. Afterwards the offers just poured in.'

And Grappelli the *grand maître*, the globetrotter?

'Oh dear, how do you try to sum up a person like Steph? Well, musically phenomenal. When we played ballads he could make you want to cry. And of course he played the swingy things and made them go like a rocket. Also that tone of his. I've hardly ever heard a classical player with such a pure tone. Okay, by saying that I'm now wide open to be shot at, but that's my honest opinion. No matter how fast the tune is played, his tone remains sublime.

At the same time one had to get used to his incredibly quick temper. It can flare up within seconds. I wasn't often on the receiving end, because it was nearly always caused by something going wrong on the organisational side, which seldom involved me. But I soon knew when to keep calm and quiet and what not to say. He never gave me any what I'd call real stick. There were little things sometimes. Oh, and there was the business about my dumping *Satin Doll*. It's a marvellous Ellington composition, but really I'd played it every night for over a year. Including the corny ending which he liked because it was successful and I couldn't stand.

Another time, I remember, I had to *beg* him to include *The Rest Of Your Life* in our programme. It seemed so obvious to me, the French connection – and I believe Michel Legrand, the composer, did once play piano for Steph. Anyway, he was adamant he didn't want to play *that tune*. Then in the end he did agree to play it, and naturally it was fantastic. But the third or fourth time we were due to play it, he made the initial announcement, this beautiful ballad and so on, and suddenly his mind went blank. Completely blank! He had to turn round to me and ask me which tune it was. *The Rest Of Your Life,* I hissed in as quiet a stage-whisper as I could manage. Of course it brought the house down! So Steph immediately did the broken Parisian bit, the *no understand,* and they absolutely loved it. So would you believe it, the next night, just about to go on, he says to me: "We play that trick again, Len. The one where we pretend to forget the name of the tune." Yes, he kept the mistake in! He could still be doing it for all I know. Cunning as a fox. . .

'His likes and dislikes? Well, he has this marvellous knowledge of history and old churches and so on. On tour it nearly always involved us in two cars. Sometimes trains, but usually the two cars: with Diz and Denny or Ike in one and I'd be with Steph in the other. Which meant opting for the scenic routes. Okay, so maybe we're on say, the A5 and he'd look over and see a village with a church-spire. We'd take an hour off and he'd buy us tea – but really it was to look inside the church. When we played in Majorca there was the chapel on the hill with a lot of the original music manuscripts by Frederic Chopin. He'd lived on the island for several years with his mistress. Steph took a great interest in that.

'Plus of course there was the endless search for antiques. He had what you'd call "a heye" for the good pieces. If he came into your home he'd be looking around at everything, straightaway, and he was a real lad for the bargains. I remember when we were going to visit the Harrissons. We stopped at a local shop which had a tray of oddments outside, including a pile of plates for 25p each. Oh, old British Railways plates, a Granny's oven plate, most of them chipped or cracked. Well, Steph went through them as if shuffling a pack of cards. There were a couple he wanted, but the guy in the shop insisted he had to take the lot. He just wanted to get rid of them. So there was a bit of an argument, a haggle, but in the end Steph did take them, all of them – with a grumble to me about "these thieves". And don't forget, here was a guy earning a lot of money per night. Then in the car he sorted out the two or three he wanted, handed me the rest – the ones he considered worthless junk – and asked me if I'd like to give them to my wife! I was left throwing them one at a time out of the passenger-window. Great Britain's next discus champion. . .

'Yes – it's all beginning to come back into my head again, the touring with Steph. For instance, the way at the end of a show he'd spend at least ten minutes rubbing the fiddle down. He'd use a silk scarf. It was a bit like an athlete, running that extra half-lap after the race. The cooling-off period, you know. He paid more attention to cleaning his instrument, the strings and the body, than any other violinist I've personally ever seen – and I've worked with a lot of them. He travelled with two violins. The Gagliano, made in Naples in 1742, and another, lesser one. But really I couldn't spot the difference. He made them both sound good.

'He didn't like to socialise much after the job. I mean most musicians need to unwind once they've played, and if there's a party on the go, well, that's the easiest way to do it. But Steph liked to get away, to eat and then go to bed. He also insisted upon having his "lie in" in the mornings. The times I've heard all that shouting and then some poor girl, a maid running off down the corridor nearly in tears because she'd tried to go in and clean the room – and Steph would be in bed still, sitting there awake and writing his letters, but not ready to get up. . .

'The only occasions he would socialise after a gig were if he'd been particularly perceptive about who it was. There was one job in Yorkshire, near Barnsley. We'd played this really rather scruffy hall, but afterwards there was a very smart, attractive lady standing with the other people hoping to get Steph's autograph. And suddenly she invited the whole group back for supper. To everyone's surprise Steph said yes, but immediately. He did the finger under the eye bit to me and said, "I know, I know." And of course he was right. We were driven up into the stockbroker belt, the house was marvellous, her supper superb and the people there really nice. Also though, I seem to recall Steph coming away holding yet another small souvenir of our visit. A couple of leather-bound, hand-tooled books, with the lettering stamped on in goldleaf. He'd obviously had his eye on them from the moment we walked in. He could be totally persevering if there was an antique or some other object he'd spotted and wanted. Persevering – and naturally it was done with all the charm in the world. He once told me he'd read of how the late old Queen Mary would visit different friends or VIPs and so admire a teaset or a piece of China or porcelain that the host and hostess felt compelled to make her a gift of it when she left. And that's exactly how Steph operated. "Oh, I like that," he'd say. "I really do like that!" Then you knew he'd leave with it. . .

'I've told you already that he loved his eating. And especially Stilton cheese. He used to ask for it everywhere we went – and he'd get quite angry if the restaurant didn't have it. However, that was storm-stations, battle positions. Charm and persuasion one minute, bad temper the next – if the charm hadn't worked. Then all over and forgotten. Which is another amazing feature of his playing. I've seen him in an absolute froth of a rage, off the set, and usually with one certain party. Maybe the booking of our hotel had gone wrong or something. Anyway, whatever it was there'd be enough for him to bite on. And he'd walk onto the stage still in this steaming temper. But then the moment he started to play it would be like the sound of an angel. *That*, I think, was a combination of his sheer professionalism and his inherent artistry. How he coped with it all. There were nights when Diz's tuning would be out with Denny's or Ike's, so he'd turn around to me, still with a broad smile on his face for the audience's sake, and he'd be saying out of the corner of his mouth, "What the hell are they up to, these two?" Only the language was a lot stronger than that!

A club date.

(Photo courtesy Lean Skeat)

'He could come out with the most outrageous, funny things – right in the middle of a performance. Once, again I think in Yorkshire, we were playing in a big village-hall and it was packed, to the very edge of the stage, which was low anyway. The people were virtually touchable. We were set up in our usual horseshoe shape, and into the middle of this beautiful ballad peformance, when suddenly – just as the guitars took over – Steph turns to me and he says: "Look at that woman in the front row. Isn't she the most ugliest woman you have ever seen?" So naturally I followed his gaze, and she was in the front row and she was ugly, but at that moment she was looking directly at me – and perhaps had even overheard what he'd said. Terrible it was, because then I didn't know where to look. He'd dropped me right in it!'

At which point I had to switch off the interviewing-machine and we just fell about laughing. Obviously with his memory in full flood, Mister Skeat was adding an almost Proustian accumulation of detail to what those tours in the mid-1970s were all about.

'Following this,' he goes on, 'we went to play a series of dates in Ireland – and that was when Steph met up with the customs-officer who was like the principal person in every Irish joke you've ever heard. We'd been playing in Dublin. Which was something else, yes. Because Stephane had been the only jazz musician, ever, to make the front page of the *Irish Times*. So that culturally, socially and in every other way the entire country had been talking about him. Well, we were coming back through the customs – and of course at that time the IRA thing had escalated to the point of being a total security worry. They were checking everything in the luggage, really stripping us off. And I'm, sort of, along the counter, getting my bags done – when suddenly I hear this "Are you kidding? Are you kidding?" from Steph. And then he pulls my sleeve, and remember we're talking there in front of this customs-man with all his gold braid and the peaked cap. But Steph says: "Do you know what this .... [author's deletion] wants me to do? He wants me to take the front off the violin!" Obviously the guy thought the front unscrewed or something. I know it sounds hideously untrue – and Irish – but he really expected to be able to look inside it. . .'

Was the violinist generally against authority, always having skirmishes with officials and so on?

'No, not really. Only if they were pompous or over-bureaucratic.

70

And of course with hotel managements and staff if things went wrong. I've told you about the maids – trying to go in his room and clean, because they had their set routines. But also if something had gone wrong with the breakfast he'd ordered – then all of a sudden there'd be this outburst of abuse from one of the rooms, his naturally, and the next minute the breakfast would be outside, sent back – until it had been done as he liked it. That was the main thing about the man again: he expected 100% service and if the coffee was cold, or whatever it was, then all hell broke loose.'

Perhaps though this links up with his meticulous attention to detail in any actual musical presentation. Wasn't it you, Len, who told me about his insistence on having a bath before the concert, at Lancaster University I think? Even though it delayed the start.

'The bath! Oh, yes. We started nearly an hour late in fact. Again, something had gone wrong with the travel arrangements – and I've got a feeling for the usual reasons. Anyway, it had been screwed up. This was one of those occasions when I'd gone up separately by road – and was already at the university. Then the message came through that they were going to be late. And yet the audience, that whole captive audience just sat there with the maximum patience, because they wanted to hear their idol no matter how long the delay. But Steph had travelled, and he wouldn't go on before he'd first visited the hotel and relaxed in the bath. That too was professionalism in its strange kind of way. He wanted to change and he needed to feel clean before he went out there to give of his best. That was the night also when several of the students presented him with a wooden (fret-sawed) Grappelli profile, covered with badges and scripted things. I still have it around the house here somewhere. It wasn't antiquey enough for Steph – although he still made them an *Oh, you are so kind!* speech of thanks.

'Diz Disley likewise was something else in those days. However, I emphasise, this was for entirely different reasons. He was *always* notoriously late – despite the fact that he usually carried the tickets, hotel reservations and any other travel documents. Steph was forever having to nag him to get himself more organised. Best of all though was the time we were going up from Euston, and we turned up at the ticket-barrier. But no Disley, who again had the tickets. So the guy at the barrier said get on the train and sort it out later. Well, at the very last moment – *and the train is actually moving* – we see this little bow-legged figure and a white guitar-case, tear through the barrier and hurl himself into the last carriage. We were well forward, and Steph said, "I teach this so-and-so a lesson!" Then he goes and locks himself, with his case and violin, in the toilet. So when Diz, huffing and puffing, at last makes it up through the train to our carriage, we look up and say: "Where's Steph, what happened?" Well, he went deathly white, thinking the star of the show was missing and it was his responsibility to get him there. We kept it up for quite some time before Steph, roaring with laughter eventually emerged from the toilet. . .'

How about the more serious side of his nature though? Did he philosophise at all on these journeyings?

'Not in the general sense or in the form of long discussions, no. I think because he was so much of an observer when we travelled, interested in everything, all that was going on. He seemed able to take in his surroundings and the people just like food and drink. But then every once in a while he'd come out with something startling – which would make *you* sit back and think. Like the time – also on a train – and he said this so very quickly I didn't quite get it at first. A little old lady went by, bent over and frail-looking, and Steph said, "You see: she could be mine." Yes, he'd immediately related the ages. He was so with it. Afterwards, when I realised what he meant it struck me as a truly profound insight on his mind, the way it ticks. . .'

Again, I think, on how he's worked so hard and still managed to preserve himself, gaining in years but without any clear evidence of mental deterioration. For I see no real contradictions in this. Man is like the flowering branches of a tree which grow quite naturally, some short, others long. Unless of course he is pruned artificially; in war or a car crash. Similarly certain branches of a tree will just wither away, while a number remain strong and healthy until the trunk itself dies. Yet Grappelli's personal strength is even greater than this. In the knowing that his music will live on beyond him.

Chapter SIX

Intelligence alone is not enough – it cannot operate, cannot be intelligence, without an approach to the world through instinctual feeling with its possibility of knowing (the inseparable) relationships as you know when you drink it that water is cold.

ALAN WATTS, *This Is IT*

BY NOW IT was late afternoon and lights were beginning to come on in the Skeat home. His wife served us food – with a bottle of wine for me. (Len had a gig that night and he doesn't drink before he plays.) So we ate, and I sipped the good red wine and for the next half-hour or so, and as well as about Steph, we talked of the marvellous Ruby Braff 'live' recordings we'd both been involved in the week before. Three nights of the great cornettist at his absolute best; with Brian Lemon on piano, Len and Jack Parnell. Had we but known it there was soon to be a war of madness in the South Atlantic, with ships going down and lives lost. For the moment though all we knew about it were rumblings over sovereignty coming from Buenos Aires (the Falkland Islands, where were they?) Consequently, at that particular point in time the room where we were appeared an agreeable microcosm of the better side to life, given over to Ruby's tapes, the Grappelli story and, overall, the more human face of jazz.

Len's wife produced a bulky file, filled with all sorts of things relating to Stephane in the 1970s. Photographs, some posed, others in action. Informal shots taken in the dressing-room. Programmes from all over the place. And of course masses of newspaper notices and fan letters. The former vary between rave headlines such as JAZZ VIOLIN AT ITS NIMBLE BEST or GREAT GRAPPELLI OVATION and the effusive prose of the *Canberra Times* critic, Michael Foster: 'There are many recollections of great beauty: things of the senses; waves almost perfect in their shape and in the power which envelops the body surfer, sunsets over ranges such as the Kaimais

73

or the Brindabellas, the smell of a bank of violets. To these must now be added the experience of hearing Stephane Grappelli play the violin. I cannot recall hearing anything so superb in my years of fortunate listening to many fine groups.'

She also had there a brief biography of Ike Isaacs, with whom I'd produced records many years before when he sat in with Ted Heath's band. (He used to play the sessions and broadcasts but not the tours.) Still somewhat underrated as a player, he was actually born in Rangoon and came to London in 1946 when he played with trumpeter Leslie 'Jiver' Hutchison. He went on to join the BBC Show Band and became a regular on 'Guitar Club'. Later still, when I knew him, he'd become a great personal friend and admirer of the late Wes Montgomery, probably the most original guitar stylist of recent years. But his first idol was still Django. As he says, '. . . the Reinhardt recording of *Chasing Shadows* was a tremendous experience for me – it opened my eyes to where music could go.'

Ike's contributions to the Grappelli group naturally differed from those of Denny Wright. They were less explosive, more delicate and introspective. However, having once seen Australia he became so enamoured of the place that he decided to take his family out and settle there. Since when he's been the country's principal jazz soloist and teacher on guitar. (Nowadays, where it's at in Stephane's group is: Diz Disley, still there, Jack Sewing on bass

Ike Isaacs.

and playing the other guitar Martin Taylor, a young Scot who promises to develop from being good into someone quite outstanding. He has been involved with music from the age of four; and prior to Stephane had toured with his father's band as well as playing the clubs in a duo situation with Ike Isaacs.)

In the meantime though Len Skeat was polishing off the last of his fruit-cake and signalled his readiness to go on. . .

'That was a funny thing, what I said before about Steph being *with it*. He always relates to the times and to life. At the period we're speaking of, Carnaby Street was all the rage. And it was also just when his grandson, young Steph, started coming around with us. He'd be about seventeen, eighteen then, something like that. They couldn't have been more like two peas out of a pod – because not only did they share the same birthday, but they seemed absolutely identical in character and would argue like mad, on account of the fact, you know. Always squabbling: maybe if Stephane wouldn't buy the younger one a watch he wanted, things like that. However, the point I'm coming to is that young Steph was always on about clothes, the Carnaby Street gear being *It* and so forth. And then one night we just couldn't believe our eyes. I mean Stephane was always smart, but this night he turned up wearing these great high-heeled boots, wedge-boots, black with red soles, and maroon velvet trousers. "What d'you tink of tis?" he said. He'd been doing the shops along Carnaby Street all afternoon! He was very flexible in things like that. He had a good eye for colour and for fashion. He wasn't like a man of his age at all, one who generally would be expected to be more set in his ways.

'In fact this reminds me of another occasion connected with clothes. We were in Edinburgh, walking down Princes Street, when suddenly he calls out to me, "Oh, look at that!" pointing into a shop-window. Again at first I couldn't believe it. It was a women's shop, a smart outfitters with all the latest models there, coats, etc. He says: "Ah, I like that," indicating a woman's bright red tartan check coat. I thought, Jesus, here we go! So in he marches, into the shop. The assistants couldn't take in that he wanted to try this coat on. But anyway they got out one his size, he put it on – and it fitted him a treat, he looked marvellous in it. So that was that. He just had to buy it.

'I think it was that evening too, or was it in York? Yes, probably York. Anyway, we were waiting in the hotel foyer for a limousine to pick us up and take us to the concert. So Steph decided he'd do his little warm-up on the violin right there on the spot. There was no one else about, but as he's playing away, this lady steps out of the lift and walks by him, and as she passes, with a quick little movement of his hand he puts it out just as if he'd been back in his old street busking days. She sort of shook her head, startled, and hurried on. Obviously she hadn't recognised who it was – and then we all fell about. Steph found the whole thing highly amusing. Yes, the Grappelli sense of humour can be very dry, the things he comes out with. . .

'Other times he could be amusing without even realising it. As in Germany for instance, when his usual "I like that" routine tripped him up. We'd done the concert and were invited back to dinner in a restaurant which had a group playing all the old Hot Club numbers. And the waiters and waitresses were in traditional costume, including the proprietor who'd rushed back to change out of the suit he'd been wearing at the concert. So Steph does his "I like that, I like that" bit, pointing at his host's short trousers and jacket. Only this time not on the make, the subtle persuasion, but meant as a genuine compliment. Then there was much chat about the trousers having been his grandfather's, etc. But the next day, just as we were leaving the hotel, Steph found himself being presented with a set of leather hose – which the restaurant-owner had gone out and specially bought for him. It was another of those very rare moments when he was lost for words – although he quickly recovered and did his little speech of thanks. We were all killing ourselves of course. Because even allowing for his sometimes surprising sartorial changes, one can't easily imagine a Grappelli wearing leather shorts.

'Speaking purely personally now, I often found that even his actual tantrums could have me in fits. But maybe most of all the one which occurred after our concert at Carnegie Hall. That was the time we visited Niagara Falls – a trip the agent for the tour had laid on for us. All very impressive. However, the concert itself was the most enormous success – packed out, and with nearly every important jazz personality in New York sitting out there. (Afterwards I made a great gaffe by at first failing to recognise John Lewis, who'd come around to see Steph and meet the group.) But then, in all the euphoria which went with the concert, Disley has this sudden brainwave. Why not have ourselves photographed the following morning outside Carnegie Hall: in front of the billposters

(*Photo David Redfern*)

Triumph!

advertising our concert? The pictures would make marvellous publicity material, he said. Well, Steph wasn't so keen. Especially since it meant giving up his precious "lie in" – and after he'd just given his *all* on stage. In the end he allowed himself to be talked into it, but still showing much reluctance. Whereupon Diz announced he'd fix it all up, the photographer and so on.

'Well, the following day we duly assembled – including an expensive New York photographer – and took taxis to the hall. It was bloody cold, and Stephane was muffled up, cursing and swearing about the wind, in a thoroughly bad mood. So we arrive at Carnegie to take up our positions, and lo and behold! – there are the men already tearing down the bills. You can imagine the effect on Steph, of course, the sheer rage. He did the jumping up and down bit. And then Disley did a runner. With Stephane in hot pursuit. I can tell you, murder was nearly committed that day. . .'

Where else did the group go in the States?

'After Carnegie we did a fortnight at the Buddy Rich Club and we packed the place every night. Benny Goodman came, Tal Farlow, and lots of big names. Tony Bennett.'

Also there was Australia.

'Yes. And that proved heavy going to begin with. Steph first of all hadn't been keen to go. When we were in Majorca he said he wanted a break. So it took Denny Wright and myself a visit to his bedroom one morning and some urgent persuasion for him to make the tour. We simply had to lay it on the line: the dates were coming in and we needed to know whether it was on or off. In the end though, when he said yes and we got out there he absolutely loved it. And we were treated so well.

'It involved about eight weeks away altogether. And I remember distinctly Diz (who once again had the tickets) turning up late at London Airport with a plastic bag, a carrier with a pair of trousers and a single shirt in it, announcing he would shop for anything else he needed out there! Pretty crazy, eh?

'In Sydney we played extra dates because the demand for seats had been so great. They issued an LP from our Town Hall concert and we did a lot of television.'

Did you ever have any other jazz artists play with the group as guests?

'Not on the tours. But once we did a concert at the Fairfield Halls, Croydon, and Earl Hines came and did one whole set with us. He'd been recording with Stephane during the day. They played tremendously together.

'I seem to recall it was very soon after this that Steph had his raging toothache. Obviously he had one or a couple of teeth which were rotten. But he was a terrible coward about having them seen to. So Disley persuaded him to have a daily mouthwash with cider vinegar. He tried it for a while, then said he preferred to dull the throb with a drop of whisky, a single malt preferably.'

How did he relax on tour? By watching the films on TV maybe?

'I'm not fully sure. I know he's interested in films though. He used to talk about Tom Mix a lot, how he took the horse home to his lodgings. And he was a great admirer, still is I think, of Bing Crosby. He'd known him as a personal friend. But then too he'd seen so many old films when he played in the Paris movie-houses. Often six and seven times over. Yet I had to remind him that he once played tin whistle over the end of a Bogart-Bacall film (*To Have And Have Not*). Strange how he could have forgotten that. . .

'Mostly he appeared to relax over his meals. Although not always when the bill arrived. There was one time when about twenty hangers-on piled into this restaurant with us after the show. And Steph was enjoying himself ordering oxtail-soup, a grilled steak and so on. But then a bill for the whole party was slipped under his plate. "There must be some mistake!" he cried. "No, no mistake," the manager said. Well, he got out of that one by pretending to have only French money on him, and so all the hangers-on had to pay their whack.

'Just occasionally, if we were particularly relaxed, he'd talk about the early days with Django. But never for very long. There had (obviously) been a terrible clash of personalities. I mean, not just Django's disappearances – which were generally creative. But other things he did which got in the way of any sort of smooth working relationship. Like he'd go off driving a car with no licence or anything – *and* talk his way out of it when the police stopped him. All those kind of things. Steph hated the sloppiness of it. And of course he had this load of weird, typically gypsy relatives who would be turning up everywhere to con him for money. In fact, a good few of them are still around. Even when we did the German tour, in almost every city we played, some distant cousin of Django would arrive backstage. With his own crop of memories.'

Were you amazed by Stephane's actual stamina on tour?

'Oh, yes – always. And, of course, by his sheer dedication. You must remember that TV programme, *The Golden Shot,* we guested on. Well, it used to be recorded in the afternoons, and this particular afternoon there was a bomb scare. The studio was in total chaos, people rushing about everywhere. But Steph stayed as cool as a cucumber. "I survived the bombing during the war," he said, "Why should I let this thing worry me now?" However, it meant that by the time the show had been recorded we had very little time to get to our concert that night, and we were tearing along the roads and breaking all the speed limits. But he still kept his cool. And gave a marvellous performance. Stamina, yes, plus professionalism of a very high order. The temperament and the tantrums only showed when there was inefficiency around.

'The only thing physically I ever heard him complain about was in the really cold weather. During the war he'd either broken or in some way damaged a finger, I think the third finger on his playing hand, down in Devon using a garden-rake and he said the cold could still make it painful. That's all though.'

Did he ever tell you the story about the nudist colony? (It's been put about that the Quintet of the Hot Club were once hired to do a show at one, for good money, but with the proviso that they too appeared without their clothes. Then, due to a management muddle, on the night in question, when the curtains parted, Steph *et al* were absolutely starkers and the audience had turned up wearing evening dress!)

LEN: 'Yes, naturally I have heard that tale. I don't know how authentic it is. It certainly sounds a very good gag, doesn't it! But I don't know. Perhaps there's a little grain of truth in it which has been worked up and then polished over the years.'

Oddly enough Len never did get to work with Stephane in France. Otherwise though, he travelled with him to all the places in the world where jazz is normally appreciated – Belgium, Holland, Spain and so on. However: my final and favourite anecdote from these travels takes us back to Scotland again. For the want of a better title I will call it *The Idylls Of The Rug*.

'Before Ed Baxter started handling the tours, Diz did quite a lot of the booking. Which meant we sometimes ended up with quite ludicrous distances between jobs. Newcastle one night, Bournemouth the next, then back up North again. But on this particular occasion we were in Glasgow for about ten days, based in a hotel from which we'd go out and do a gig each night maybe thirty, forty miles away.

'Well, in the hotel foyer, above the stairs as you went up there was a big, old, grey-with-age rug in a glass case. I don't know whether it was Persian, Egyptian or what. But Steph's eyeball had spotted it immediately, and he turned to the agent for the tour and did his usual bit. "Oh, I like that, the rug. Do you think you could get it for me? Somehow?" So the agent in his folly and eager to keep his artist happy said, "Yes, yes, oh there's no problem about that. I'll get you the rug alright." Of course he had no right to say any such thing, but anyway he did.

'Every day after this Stephane went on at him, about the rug, and the agent kept saying, "There's no problem. I haven't seen the chap yet, but it'll be okay. You'll have it." Until it came to the very last day, the morning when we had to leave Glasgow and get ourselves down to York for another concert that night. It meant catching the one o'clock train out, and the agent was due to come with a fleet of cars to take us to the station. So now – and remember, we've done all the work for him – comes twelve o'clock and there are no cars, nothing. Well, Disley's sent to 'phone and there's no answer at the agent's number. Then suddenly it's a quarter past twelve, then it's nearly half-past and Steph's in a real rage, stamping about, going absolutely bananas, because not only has the agent let us down and we're late but he's also minus the rug. It's still in its case on the wall and there's nobody can do a thing about it.

'Well, next Diz is packed off with yet another flea in his ear to get two cabs. Oh, by the way, Ray Dempsey was the other guitarist with us, depping for Denny – and he and I took the second cab, tearing after Steph and Diz to make the train. The journey to the station was I think five miles, and we now had something like twenty-five minutes left. So we get into town, nearly there and all at once the cab in front stops. It's got a flat tyre. So there were arms and legs flying – with the driver pointing to the tyre and Steph sticking his head out and shouting "Drive on! Drive on!"

'Anyway the driver, who's in fear of all that's going on, does just that: driving with this flat tyre wobbling about, into the station approach. And so I thought we'd made it. . .

'But no! We're all clambering out of the taxis and getting our instruments out – and I could see Steph just in front wearing this very distinguished-looking Astrakhan hat. We paid both the drivers, and then we go around a corner in this enormous great station, and there, well, we simply couldn't believe our eyes! Remember he's had the nightmare cab journey. He's had the disappointment of the rug. The agent hasn't turned up. And there he is, Stephane the world star performer with his fiddle-case going up in the air, his hat askew and kicking the wretched Disley all over the place.

'We'd come to the wrong station!'

Chapter SEVEN

NEVERTHELESS THEY made the date. After another helter-skelter car ride from Glasgow to Edinburgh and a train ride down from there. Then a quick bath and yet again Stephane played magnificently. The innate professionalism had taken over from the spontaneous outbreak of anger. This is the stuff of which great performers are made. Or, as Malcolm Lowry once put it, the lighthouse invites the storm and lights it.

The man himself, the occasional balls-up notwithstanding, has no regrets about the itinerant nature of his career in jazz. 'I intend to keep playing until I drop,' he told columnist John Gibson. 'My heart is still twenty. Nothing worries me for long. Absolutely nothing. I'm nervous, you see, but I stay on top of it by moving all the time, and I can calm down quickly. I have learned that worrying gets you nowhere, so I am a bit of a fatalist. I am quite happy to live in France and travel from there. Travel for me is a great hobby. I never tire of it. What I play myself is, I like to think, a cocktail because I am influenced and impressed by so many people. But you must do your own cooking at home in jazz. . .'

However, so far we have been largely concerned with Stephane Grappelli as public performer and travelling with a regular group. There are two further aspects of his musical life which also demand to be considered. First his great interest in other, younger musicians; and secondly his various recordings with players not in his own group.

He has been particularly generous with his time and in giving encouragement to younger players, especially in the recent, busiest years. (Provided of course they have the necessary talent.) It even goes to the extent of having them make 'surprise' appearances with him onstage – and with absolutely no feelings of resentment that they might be stealing some of the limelight away from himself.

When he first arrived in Adelaide, Australia, for instance, no doubt jetlagged and wanting a bath, nevertheless he straightaway

(Photo MPS Records)

Philip Catherine.

sat down and listened keenly to three young guitarists who welcomed him with a selection of Hot Club numbers: Paul Smyth, Brian Moore and Randy Bulpin. He not only applauded them after their renditions of *Tears, Mabel* and *Sweet Chorus* – he then asked them to carry on improvising during the press interviews.

Then naturally one has to mention the young Belgian guitarist Philip Catherine. No less a jazz personage than Charles Mingus christened him 'Young Django' or the 'Django of the Seventies'. When he was nine or ten he actually stayed in the same house in Brussels (the Galerie St. Hubert) where Django used to go and play. Philip's uncle lived upstairs; Django played downstairs – and the boy's ears determined his future career. Stephane has both befriended him and of course recorded with him.

Inevitably too there have been the talented younger violinists. Jean-Luc Ponty from Avranches, Normandy, who plays both the normal and an electric violin and who has gone on to cross-fertilise jazz with rock music sounds; an amazing talent owing much of his initial inspiration and a kind of unofficial sponsorship to Grappelli.

Perhaps even more to the point is the help Steph has given to Nigel Kennedy, the Birmingham-born violinist and a product of the Yehudi Menuhin School. (Menuhin himself has become increasingly associated with Stephane's own career – on records.) Anyway, Nigel is one of the brightest new soloists on the classical circuit. But he is an avid Grappelli fan and Stephane has freely promoted him as an addition to his own shows, beginning in London and continuing on to the Edinburgh Festival where they 'jammed' together on *Ain't Misbehavin'*, *Lady Be Good* and *Sweet Sue*.

Jack Hobbs, publisher (of Spike Milligan among others) and jazz piano player, has several revealing memories of Nigel, of Yehudi and, very clearly of Stephane.

'In fact, it was Stephane who indirectly brought about my début on piano at the Royal Festival Hall,' he told me.

'Several years ago I received a telephone call one Friday evening. It went something like this:
Hello, is that Jack Hobbs?
Yes.
This is Yehudi Menuhin here.
What does one say? *Oh – really.*
Most people say that, but it really is me.
What can I do for you then?
Well, we have a mutual friend called Alan Clare.
Indeed.
And he gave me your name. You see every year we have a concert at the Festival Hall to raise money for the Menuhin School. All the pupils perform and this year one of my pupils, Nigel Kennedy aged sixteen is going to open the second half by playing jazz violin. His new passion was inspired by the visit recently to the school of Stephane Grappelli.
I see. But where do I come in?
Well, Alan Clare was going to accompany Nigel, since he usually accompanies Stephane. Unfortunately he's ill, but he said you could do it without a bass-player since you swing very well. Will you do it?
Yes, of course. When is it?
Tomorrow!

Nigel Kennedy, Yehudi Menuhin, Jack Hobbs.

'Instant terror, but too late to back down. However, I went to the school that evening, met Nigel and we had a little rehearsal. He was superb. It didn't matter what I played, he was there on key and timing. I began to feel more confident.

'On Saturday, in velvet finery and floppy bow-tie, appropriate I thought to my one and only Festival Hall appearance, I sat in the audience watching the performances. The brilliance of the Menuhin students took my breath away, and I grew more and more nervous glancing around at the well-heeled, dinner-jacketed audience.

'In the interval I went to the Green Room. Nigel was there. We rehearsed the intro and the ending again, more for my benefit than his.

'Yehudi looked at me. *Are you alright?* he asked. *Not very*, I said, slightly tremolo. Yehudi as is well-known does not drink or smoke. He smiled at me. *Go to the end of the corridor*, he said. *You will find a bar there. Tell them to give you a large vodka-and-tonic and put it down to me. When you come back stand here in the wings. I will be on-stage talking about raising money, which is why you are here. You will hear your name – then walk out to the piano. Do not look to the right for that is where* They *are. Imagine there is a beer on the piano, count four and start.*

'*Nigel will be there*, he pointed. *And I will be here at the side of the piano.*

'Horrified, I gasped: *But you'll hear all the bad chords and mistakes!*

'He smiled reassuringly. They *won't notice*, he pointed again. *And I have heard them all before!*

'I have never played *Sweet Georgia Brown* so well in my life, thanks to the understanding and kindliness of Yehudi Menuhin, the brilliance of a then sixteen-year-old Nigel and not least to Stephane Grappelli himself: whose fault it all was in the first place!'

Thanks to the extreme thoroughness of Tony Middleton's discography – and Stephane's recording career has been particularly prolific as well as long – there is no need for me to start listing all the names he has worked with in settings away from those of his own group. Nor do I want to go into any very detailed musical analysis since all of the records have been reviewed many times over. I have made my evaluation of his sound and style and other jazz qualities in the earlier part of the book and must now stand by what has been said.

However, even with these thoughts in mind, there are – I hope – still a few useful comments to be made on the subject of his records with fellow-luminaries.

The first being his ability to fit in with such a variety of different talents and still be himself; yet conveying an impression of having known their musical work intimately over a long period of time and knowing exactly how to agree with it. It came as a complete surprise to me when I acquired Paul Simon's first solo album after his split with Art Garfunkel (an outstanding album which includes his *Mother And Child Reunion* and *Me And Julio Down By The Schoolyard*) and then discovered a track with Grappelli on it. But no, there it is: one minute and twenty seconds called *Hobo's Blues*, and with the pop/folk star and guitarist dutifully accompanying someone he had clearly been an admirer of for years.

Another thing which has to be said is how *quickly* as well as easily Steph fits in with other great players of jazz. They can be as contrasting as Earl Hines and Oscar Peterson, Slam Stewart and Barney Kessel. But there is a quality of being able to seize the moment about Stephane's contributions. For financial and other reasons, like not liking to be tied down and preferring the actual organisation of a recording to be flexible, in recent years he has flatly refused to sign any exclusive contracts with one record company. Which in turn gives him the opportunity to record with many different players. On the other hand this does mean that most of his sessions are hastily arranged affairs. Nevertheless, he always seems to remain on top of the situation. Always clear, always the same Stephane and with the ability to perform in easy tandem with whoever it is, no matter what their style or temperament.

This seems an appropriate point to quote Jack Hobbs again.

'It was quite a few years ago, maybe twelve or so, when Terry Hennebury was recording some marvellous jazz programmes for BBC Television. In one historic week many famous jazzmen appeared at Ronnie Scott's club to be recorded for the series. Joe Venuti, Lionel Hampton, Buck Clayton, Red Norvo and many others graced the premises with their brilliance.

'One afternoon during this particular week I was in London and called in to see an old friend of mine, Doug Dobell at his record shop. He was just leaving. "I'm going to Ronnie Scott's to watch a BBC rehearsal," he said, "would you like to come?" It seemed like a good idea. It turned out to be a better idea than I had expected, for this was the first meeting of Stephane Grappelli and that fine ex-Benny Goodman pianist Teddy Wilson. I watched fascinated as these two great jazzmen, with no previous rehearsal or even conference, counted four beats and plunged, at incredible speed, into the most dynamic version of *Lady Be Good* that I have ever heard. The musical marriage between the two was perfect from the very first note. Needless to say, the whole afternoon passed by quickly and enjoyably. The sadness came later.

'These programmes were shown late at night on BBC 2 and there must have been something like thirty hours of recordings of these great stars, many of them now dead. I doubt if more than a fifth of

Niels-Henning Ørsted-Pedersen.   Larry Coryell.

the material was shown, and I learnt afterwards that due to its policy at the time of stringent economy, the BBC in its infinite wisdom wiped nearly all of the tapes so that they could be used again for recording. (They also obliterated Hancock for all time by the same method.) What a loss to the world, the BBC, the video industry, not to mention the loss of continuing PRS royalties for the artists, which I am sure would please Stephane not one little bit!'

Obviously with so much material to pick and choose from one has to have purely personal favourites. I've enjoyed living with all of the Grappelli/Reinhardt collaborations since transferred to LP; despite the recording imperfections of some of the earlier items. And I enjoy them for the compositions almost as much as the playing. Clashes of personality aside, when they were really flying together it proved magical. Perhaps they did strike sparks off one another. Who cares? What the sparks then ignited is unique in jazz.

I've already mentioned the 'Young Django' LP made with Philip Catherine, Larry Coryell and the tremendous bass-player from Denmark, Niels-Henning Ørsted-Pedersen. The sheer beauty with which Stephane handles the melody line of Philip's *Galerie St.-Hubert,* the cheeky dexterity of *Oriental Shuffle* and above all his

88

Bach-like grandeur on *Minor Swing*. These for me are standouts even by Grappelli standards. No wonder at the end Larry Coryell shouts his praises. Steph added more modestly: 'Maybe it was good.'

I also like very much the 'Reunion' LP with George Shearing, 'Giants' with Shearing again and Jean-Luc Ponty and 'Afternoon In Paris' with Marc Hemmeler on piano and Kenny Clarke on drums. Then of course there's the set of duets with his original inspiration, Joe Venuti. And I wouldn't like to be without the 1978 LP with Roland Hanna and Bucky Pizzarelli (George Duvivier on bass and Oliver Jackson, drums). The tunes are all familiar except Pizzarelli's delicate *Strayhorn: The Lady Is A Tramp, Sweet Chorus, Sweet And Lovely, Louise*. But Hanna plays some of the most joyously swinging piano ever heard in Grappelli's company, while Pizzarelli on guitar avoids all overt references to Django and just concentrates on being his own very good self.

Quite deliberately I have left the Grappelli-Menuhin sessions until last. Largely because with these duets (and there are now quite

Left to right: Oliver Jackson, Roland Hanna, SG, George Duvivier, Bucky Pizzarelli.

(Photo Black & Blue Records)

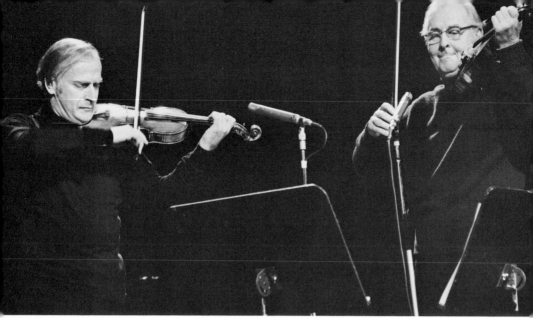

Yehudi and Stephane rehearse for the Parkinson Show.

Yehudi, Alan Clare, Stephane.

a lot of them) the two great violinists have entered a whole new dimension in public popularity, capturing the imagination of masses of people who wouldn't normally stop to listen to them as individuals. Classical followers of Menuhin have been amazed by the natural ease of his partnership with Grappelli. Jazz *aficionados* have now accepted him as a desirable convert. And yet their teaming needn't be all that surprising. Yehudi has always demonstrated musical interests way beyond Elgar and the Beethoven Violin Concerto. He has studied and played with the Indian sitar masters, for instance. While his own autobiography is really a globetrotter's guide to other and diverse musical cultures.

Meanwhile though: he has very kindly written to me about his first encounter with Stephane.

'The BBC rang me on Christmas morning ten years ago and said I must come that evening and play live on television with Stephane Grappelli. I replied that I admired him very much indeed – the wife of a former director of the Royal Festival Hall, who knew Stephane, had sent me some of his records – but I came to the television studios with some trepidation, as this was a totally unfamiliar field of music for me. The only jazz record I knew was *Jealousy,* because my sisters and I had tango lessons to that in 1935!

'White with fear I went before the cameras and played live with Stephane, and to my delight I survived intact. French television was extremely jealous and within two days had a team on my doorstep, demanding that we do the same for them! We subsequently made our first recording, and over the years have become close friends. Stephane's gift for improvisation is absolutely unique and his sheer musicality never fails to move me.'

Appropriately 'Jealousy' was the title of the album which followed their initial appearance together on TV (with Alan Clare again leading the support group). Since when there have been fairly regular reunions on disc, the most recent being a collection of Irving Berlin songs scored by Frank Sinatra's main musical director, Nelson Riddle. However 'Jealousy' and the other earlier collections had arrangements by Max Harris. So it was to him that I went for this, the book's final interview on the life and music of Stephane Grappelli.

'Yes, it first of all came about when I got a call from the production office for the Parkinson Show, he told me. 'I suppose really I'd been thought of because of the dual nature thing, being a

(Photo Reg Wilson)

Stephane, Yehudi, Max Harris, Lennie Bush, Ronnie Verrell.
Recording for EMI.

jazzman but also able to write for strings. Afterwards it seemed the logical course, to go on and make records.

'Being a pianist, I felt an additional affinity with Steph, because he's certainly no slouch in that direction either. If something ever happens to his violin elbow, he could still make an impressive contribution at the keyboard. In fact, I was the one who generally urged him to play a bit of Fats Waller for us at the end of the sessions.

'As regards the violin duets though, each man seemed to know instinctively what should be done. Very rarely would one turn to the other and suggest any alteration in what they were playing. They were both remarkably quick in picking up things. Which made life easier for me. When I was commissioned to do the first arrangements, I remember an executive at the BBC said to be careful what I put down for Stephane because he was a jazzman. In other words, don't write anything too difficult! Of course, when the time came Steph proved just as fast a reader as Yehudi. Steph actually would read the score and then commit it to memory, subsequently playing with his eyes closed and building on the part as he went along.'

So then you progressed to the recordings?

'That's right. I wrote the arrangements for four of their albums altogether.'

Each with calculated changes of personnel?

'Well, slightly – depending on availability. One of the albums had to be made in Holland. And on the last one we used a French bassist, Pierre Michelot. But the rapport between the two violins never changed. They're very different as men of course. Yehudi is the strict one. Doesn't drink or smoke and is into all the health food business. Stephane is just into food! But wiry and fit for all that.

'When we did the first LP he was also playing each night at Ronnie Scott's. But still doing beautifully in the studio the following morning. And naturally I used to go along to Ronnie's to hear him play "live". Anyway – and this shows the quickness of mind he has – I was sitting there with Alan Clare when this other, rather pushy piano-player who shall be nameless asked if he could sit in on the next set. It was totally out of order. Steph was up to it though. "Well," he said, parrying the request, "okay, but you realise that first of all we would have to rehearse!"

'He didn't talk too much about the past. A little bit about Django sometimes. About how unreliable he was. On the day of a recording session they literally had to go around all the local bars to find him.

'And he'd talk about George Shearing quite a bit. About when they were playing at Hatchett's together. During the blackouts it was often George who took Stephane home! And once they were sharing a bedroom on some out-of-town gig. Stephane was trying to sleep when suddenly, in the dark, he hears this great roar of laughter coming from George. Alarmed, he switched on the light and there's George sitting up in bed and thoroughly enjoying some story in Braille!'

Which in turn reminds me of another anecdote attributed to Shearing. Someone had made him the present of a cheese-grater. Asked about it later, he replied, 'Well, do you know, it has to be the most violent book I've ever read. . .'

MAX: 'Often I'd give Steph a lift back to his place after the sessions. Although he once cracked that now he was over sixty-five he didn't mind going on the buses because he only had to pay half-price!

'He hated getting involved with contracts. "Can't we leave that till later," he'd say. And VAT was his *bête noire*. English VAT especially.'

Was he pretty quick at the sessions in identifying mistakes?

'Yes, extremely quick. He has a marvellous ear, of course. Obviously too he'd say something if the tempo wasn't quite right for him. Otherwise I found him the easiest person to work in conjunction with. His rehearsals were usually just as good as the performances. He didn't like to do too many takes – and he would show annoyance if for other, technical reasons we had to go to say, a take four. He said he could feel all the inspiration going out of his playing. The last LP I did with him was digital, and at that time there was no really effective way of editing the tape. Which meant extra, full-length performances – and I think then he got tetchy because, quite rightly, he felt the music was becoming secondary to the equipment. It was only at our earliest sessions that he worried about the balance between the two violins, and their different sounds – probably because Yehudi has the famous Strad. But once he'd heard it was okay he never interfered on that side again.

'The routinings [preparations] were very straightforward. I'd be told what the numbers were and then it was merely a question of sorting out a good key for him to play in. Yehudi didn't involve himself in this. He trusted Stephane implicitly. But he then wanted to have his parts in advance of the sessions. Not because he felt insecure with jazz, but because he wanted to put in his own distinctive bowing marks for the thematic passages. He was extra-careful over this. By the time we recorded them his manuscripts looked like paintings!

'Going back to Stephane briefly though. He's marvellous in the way he just keeps on improving. The style doesn't change all that much, but the flair's always there. And the tone. The most tremendous tone ever heard from a jazz violin player. Meanwhile the improvisation and the phrasing just get better and better.

'He's admired by every musician, every other violinist. At the last session I did with him, we had a larger string section than usual – and there were some very distinguished faces, the cream of the London session scene. Men you'd think had seen and heard it all. Even so, at the end they gave him a standing ovation.

'He's become the most famous European jazzman of all time. Beyond dispute. So that's it: end of story. . .'

(Photo Tim Motion)

Against London's rooftops. 'Sitting On Top Of The World'.

We think we recognise someone in passing. A mistake? But then a moment later we bump into them. The preview was merely our arrival on their wavelength – within their magnetic orbit. My concluding thought about Stephane is actually still my first: that he has been, is one of the most easily recognisable figures in the whole history of music. Once heard, never forgotten. In a sense, and rather like the late Bill Evans on piano, he is a natural phenomenon that jazz was always feeling its way towards. But once the two met, so the instrument itself changed – until now we cannot conceive of the violin without him.

Years ago, when I first reviewed records on a regular basis, I would find myself disappointed if there wasn't anything good to be said. Destructive criticism is not my line. In addition, I happen to believe that the only justification for a writing about music is to help promote it. Before being invited to do this profile of Grappelli, I'd already turned down the chance to write about someone else in jazz. Simply because I couldn't work up enough enthusiasm. Well, this certainly cannot be said of Stephane. And now I'm reluctant to let him go. So: I think I'll just go into the next room and put a record on. Which one though? I'd better consult Tony's discography. . . .

Mount Felix, 1982

Introduction to the discography

This discography is divided into two parts comprising recordings issued under Stephane Grappelly's name in the period 1940 to 1947 and all known recordings made for commercial issue from 1954 to date. Not included are recordings with Django Reinhardt as these have been well documented in 'DJANGO REINHARDT' by Charles Delauny published in 1981 by Ashley Mark Company. Also excluded is Grappelly's work with Hatchett's Swingtette. For his collaboration with Django I would highly recommend the following LPs Decca Ace of Clubs ACL1185, ACL1189, Eclipse ECM2051 and a selection of his recordings with Hatchett's Swingtette are represented on Decca Recollections RFL11. In my endeavours I am most grateful to the eminent French discographer and record label researcher Michel Ruppli who supplied me with so much information on recordings made in France and whose discography of Stephane Grappelli in the French periodical 'Jazz Hot' was the inspiration for my efforts. Also my thanks to discographical colleague Alan Newby and musicians Joe Deniz, Allan Ganley and Ray Swinfield. I have consulted the major discographical works particularly those of Brian Rust and Jorgen Grunnet Jepsen plus numerous other publications and record catalogues. Regarding the spelling of Stephane's surname, in earlier years it was normally ended with 'y', in the late sixties 'i' replaced the 'y' and thus appears in the discography. The following abbreviations have been used to indicate the country of record issue – (E) United Kingdom, (F) France, (G) West Germany, (US) U.S.A., (Au) Australia. Where no abbreviation is used records issued in the U.K.

Tony Middleton
London, December 1982

97

STEPHANE GRAPPELLY AND HIS MUSICIANS　　　　　　　　*London, July 30, 1940*
Stephane Grappelly (*solo violin*), Stanley Andrews (*violin*), Harry Chapman (*harp*), Reg
Conroy (*vibes*), George Shearing (*piano*), Jack Llewellyn (*guitar*), Hank Hobson (*bass*), Al
Philcock (*drums*)

DR4902-2	*I never knew*	Decca unissued
DR4903-2	*After you've gone*	Decca F7570, MOR530, Ace of Clubs
		ACL1121
DR4904-2	*Stephane's tune*	Decca F7570

London, February 28, 1941
Stephane Grappelly (*solo violin*), Eugene Pini/Stanley Andrews (*violins*), Dennis Moonan
(*violin, alto*), unknown (*cello*), Harry Chapman (*harp*), George Shearing (*piano*), Syd Jacobson
(*guitar*), George Gibbs (*bass*), Jock Jacobson (*drums*)

DR4902-3	*I never knew*	Decca F8128, TAB55
DR5403-1	*Sweet Sue, just you*	Decca F7841　　—
DR5404-2	*Tiger rag*	Decca F7787
DR5405-2	*Stephane's blues*	Decca F7787
DR5406-1	*Noel brings the swing*	Decca F7841　　—

STEPHANE GRAPPELLY AND HIS QUARTET　　　　　　　　*London, April 9, 1941*
Stephane Grappelly (*violin*), George Shearing (*piano*), Jack Llewellyn (*guitar*), George Gibbs
(*bass*), Dave Fullerton (*drums*)

DR5579-1	*Dinah*	Decca F7865, MOR530, TAB55
DR5580-2	*Liza*	Decca unissued
DR5581-1	*Body and soul*	Decca F8128, MOR530, Ace of Clubs
		ACL1121
DR5582-1	*Jive bomber*	Decca F7865, TAB55

STEPHANE GRAPPELLY AND HIS QUINTET　　　　　　*London, February 17, 1942*
Stephane Grappelly (*violin*), Pat Dodd (*piano*), Chappie D'Amato/Joe Deniz (*guitars*), Tommy
Bromley (*bass*), Dave Fullerton (*drums, vocal*)

DR6685-2	*Margie*	Decca F8175, MOR530
DR6686-2	*You're the cream in my coffee*	Decca F8175, MOR530
DR6687-2	*Nagasaki*	Decca unissued
DR6688-2	*I'm coming Virginia*	Decca unissued
	(Grappelli plays piano)	

STEPHANE GRAPPELLY AND HIS QUINTET　　　　　　*London, August 20, 1942*
Stephane Grappelly (*violin*), Roy Marsh (*vibes*), Pat Dodd (*piano*), Chappie D'Amato/Joe
Deniz (*guitars*), Tommy Bromley (*bass*), Dave Fullerton (*drums, vocal*)

DR6930-2	*Liza*	Decca F8204
DR6931-2	*Hallelujah*	Decca unissued
DR6932-2	*Sleepy Lagoon*	Decca unissued
DR6933-2	*The folks who live on the hill*	
	vDF	Decca F8204

Stephane Grappelli did occasional dates with his own group while still at Hatchett's and the
following musicians worked with him during the early part of 1943. Arthur Penn (*baritone*),
George Shearing or Jack Penn (*piano*), Chappie D'Amato/Bert Weedon (*guitars*), Joe
Nussbaum (*bass*), Dave Fullerton (*drums*). Some of these may be the unknown musicians on
the next Decca session.

STEPHANE GRAPPELLY AND HIS QUINTET *London, January 28, 1943*
Stephane Grappelly (*violin*), unknown (*baritone*), George Shearing (*piano*), unknown (*guitars*), unknown (*bass*), Dave Fullerton (*drums, vocal*)

DR7187-	*Ain't she sweet?* vDF	Decca unissued
DR7188-	*I'll never be the same*	Decca unissued
DR7189-2	*Stardust*	Decca F8451, MOR530, TAB55
DR7190-2	*Au revoir (J'Attendrai)*	Decca F8451, TAB55

STEPHANE GRAPPELLY AND HIS QUINTET *London, July 7, 1943*
Stephane Grappelly (*violin*), George Shearing (*piano*), Chappie D'Amato/Joe Deniz (*guitars*), Tommy Bromley (*bass*), Dave Fullerton (*drums, vocal*), Beryl Davis (*vocal*)

DR7386-	*Weep no more, my lady* vBD	Decca F8333
DR7387-	*When I look at you* vBD	Decca F8334
DR7388-	*Three o'clock in the morning*	Decca F8334
DR7389-	*That old black magic* vBD	Decca F8333

Stephane Grappelli left Hatchett's in August 1943 to work fulltime with his own group. George Shearing (*piano*), Joe Deniz (*solo guitar*), Alan Mindell/Laurie Deniz (*guitars*), Lou Nussbaum (*bass*), Dave Fullerton (*drums, vocal*), Beryl Davis (*vocal*). Some of these may be the unknown musicians on the following Decca sessions.

STEPHANE GRAPPELLY AND HIS QUARTET *London, October 6, 1943*
Stephane Grappelly (*violin*), George Shearing (*piano*), unknown (*guitars*), unknown (*bass*), Dave Fullerton (*drums, vocal*), Beryl Davis (*vocal*)

DR7727-	*Strictly non-vocal*	Decca unissued
DR7728-2	*Star eyes* vBD	Decca F8375
DR7729-2	*Heavenly music* vBD	Decca F8375
DR7730-	*She's funny that way* vDF	Decca unissued

London, December 3, 1943

Stephane Grappelly (*violin*), George Shearing (*piano*), unknown (*guitars*), unknown (*bass*), Dave Fullerton (*drums, vocal*), Beryl Davis (*vocal*)

DR7926-	*Baby please stop and think about me* vBD,DF	Decca unissued
DR7927-2	*I never mention your name, oh no* vDF	Decca F8392
DR7928-2	*My heart tells me* vDF	Decca F8392
DR7929-	*Ol' man river*	Decca unissued

Stephane Grappelli reformed his group early in 1944. George Shearing (*piano*), Alan Mindell/Denny Wright (*guitars*), Arthur O'Neill (*bass*), Dave Fullerton (*drums*), Gloria Brent (*vocal*)

STEPHANE GRAPPELLY AND HIS SEXTET *London, June 10, 1944*
Stephane Grappelly (*violin*), George Shearing (*piano*), unknown (*guitars*), Arthur O'Neill(?) (*bass*), Dave Fullerton (*drums*), Beryl Davis (*vocal*)

DR8527-	*Ain't misbehavin'*	Decca unissued
DR8528-	*I found a new baby*	Decca unissued
DR8529-	*Confessin'* vBD	London(US)155
DR8530-	*Someday sweetheart* vBD	Decca F9745

Group disbanded for a few months. In November 1944 Stephane Grappelli fronted the Tommy Hunt Orchestra for a one nighter tour.

STEPHANE GRAPPELLY AND HIS QUARTET/QUINTET   *London, November 29, 1944*
Stephane Grappelly (*violin*), George Shearing (*piano*), Alan Mindell/Denny Wright (*guitars*),
Arthur O'Neill (*bass*), Dave Fullerton (*drums*), Beryl Davis (*vocal*)

DR8901-	*Henderson stomp*	Decca F9745, MOR530
DR8902-	*Don't you know that I care?*	
	vBD	Decca F8492, London(US)101
DR8903-	*No-one else will do* vBD	Decca F8492, London(US)101
DR8904-	*Jam sandwich*	Decca unissued

Stephane Grappelli fronted a small group at Bates Club, London February to July 1945. Alan
Hodgkins (*guitar*), Tommy Bromley (*bass*), Dave Fullerton (*drums, vocal*), Edna Kaye (*vocal*)

STEPHANE GRAPPELLY   *London, May 13, 1945*
Stephane Grappelly (*violin*), Arthur Young (*piano*), other details unknown. Beryl Davis (*vocal*)

DR9419-	*Sentimental nocturne*	Decca unissued
DR9420-	*Who's koo koo?*	Decca unissued
DR9421-	*I'm beginning to see the light*	Decca unissued
DR9422-	*Candy*	Decca unissued

STEPHANE GRAPPELLY AND HIS ORCHESTRA   *London, October 25, 1945*
Stephane Grappelly (*violin*), unknown (*strings*), George Shearing (*piano*), unknown (*guitar*),
unknown (*bass*), Dave Fullerton(?) (*drums*), Doreen Henry (*vocal*)

DR9762-2	*Sugar* vDH	Decca F8582
DR9763-1	*(You came along from)*	
	out of nowhere	Decca F8582
DR9764-	*Wendy*	Decca unissued

STEPHANE GRAPPELLY AND HIS QUARTET   *London, October 25, 1945*
Stephane Grappelly (*violin*), George Shearing (*piano*), unknown (*bass*), Dave Fullerton(?)
(*drums*)

DR9765-	*Piccadilly stomp*	Decca unissued

STEPHANE GRAPPELLY QUINTET   *London, April 25, 1947*
Stephane Grappelly (*violin*), George Shearing (*piano*), Dave Goldberg(?) (*guitar*), Coleridge
Goode (*bass*), Ray Ellington (*drums*)

DR11185-	*Yellow house stomp*	Decca F8917
DR11186-	*Red-O-Ray*	Decca F8917
DR11187-	*Channel crossing*	Decca unissued
DR11188-	*In the mode* (Mood)	Decca unissued

STEPHANE GRAPPELLY'S HOT FOUR   *Paris, October 17, 1947*
Stephane Grappelly (*violin*), Joseph Reinhardt/Roger Chaput (*guitars*), Emmanuel Soudieux
(*bass*)

OSW478-1	*Oui pour vous revoir*	Swing(F)SW271, Pathé(F)2C054-16028
OSW479-	*Soleil d'automne*	Swing unissued

Stephane Grappelly (*piano solos*)   *Paris, October 17, 1947*

OSW480-	*Bebop Medley*	Swing unissued
OSW481-1	*Tea for two*	Swing(F)SW271, Pathé(F)2C054-16028

STEPHANE GRAPPELLY TRIO   *Paris, May 1954*
Stephane Grappelly (*piano*), Guy Pederson (*bass*), Baptiste 'Mac Kac' Reilles (*drums*)

Viens au creux de mon épaule	CFD(F)45, Musidisc(F)30JA5216	
Lookin' at you	—	—
I can't recognize the tune	—	—
Red-O-Ray	—	—
Crazy Blues	—	—
Marno	—	—

Omit drums   *Paris, May 1954*

Tendrement (Tenderly)	CFD(F)45, Musidisc(F)30JA5216	
Vous qui passez sans me voir	—	—
Wendy	—	—
Valse du passé	—	—

CFD = Club Français du Disque, title: *Piano à Gogo*. Musidisc title: *Unique piano session Paris 1955*

JACK DIEVAL AVEC STEPHANE GRAPPELLY   *Paris, September 17, 1954*
Stephane Grappelly (*violin*), Jack Dieval (*piano*), Benoît Quersin (*bass*), Jean-Louis Viale (*drums*)

A gal in Calico	HMV(F)FFLP1042, VSM(F)7EMF65	
Pennies from heaven	—	—
The world is waiting for the sunrise	—	—
Can't help lovin' that man	—	
I can't recognize the tune	—	
You took advantage of me	—	
The folks who live on the hill	—	

Note: Stephane Grappelly does not play on *Louise*, the one other title from the above LP

Title: *Jazz aux Champs-Elysées No.2*

HENRI CROLLA-STEPHANE GRAPPELLY QUARTET   *Paris, December 30, 1954*
Stephane Grappelly (*violin*), Henri Crolla (*guitar*), Emmanuel Soudieux (*bass*), Mac Kac (*drums*)

Swing 93	Ducretet-Thompson(F)250V004	
Belleville	—	
Manoir de mes rêves	—	
Djangology	—	460V068
Alembert's	Ducretet-Thompson(F)255V005	—
Just can't be love		—
Have you met Miss Jones?		—

Stephane Grappelly (*piano*), other personnel as previous   *Paris, December 30, 1954*

Marno	Ducretet-Thompson(F)260V041

250V004 = Ducretet-Thompson(E)D93067

STEPHANE GRAPPELLY   *Paris, April 12, 1955*
Stephane Grappelly (*violin*), Michel Hausser (*vibes*), Maurice Vander (*piano*), René Duchaussoir (*guitar*), Benoît Quersin (*bass*), Jean-Louis Viale (*drums*)

26102	*Night and day*	Barclay(F)74006, 84006, 8109213		
26103	*Aime-moi*	—		
26104	*The nearness of you*	—	—	—
26105	*Don't worry about me*	—	—	—

Stephane Grappelly (*violin*), Maurice Vander (*piano*), Benoît Quersin (*bass*), Jean-Louis Viale (*drums*)

26870	*Birth of the blues*	Barclay(F)84006, 8109213	
26871	*Lover man*	—	
26872	*Lady be good*	—	—
26873	*I can't believe that you're in love with me*	—	
26874	*Tangerine*	—	

Barclay 84006 = Felsted(E)PDL 86048

Paris, February 6, 1956

Stephane Grappelly (*violin*), Maurice Vander (*piano*), Pierre Michelot (*bass*), Mac Kac (*drums*)

30231	*Dans la vie*	Barclay(F)84034		
30232	*Fascinatin' rhythm*	—	, 8109213, EmArcyMG36120	
30233	*Time after time*	—	—	
30234	*S'wonderful*	—	—	—

Same   *Paris, February 14, 1956*

30379	*Taking a chance on love*	Barclay(F)84034, 8109213, EmArcy(US)MG36120	
30380	*Cheek to cheek*	—	—
30381	*Slow en re majeur*	—	
30382	*She's funny that way*	—	—	—
30383	*The lady is a tramp*	—	—	—

Maurice Vander (*harpsichord*), other personnel as last   *Paris, February 14, 1956*

30384	*Someone to watch over me*	Barclay(F)84034, 8109213, EmArcy(US)MG36120
30385	*Crazy rhythm*	Barclay unissued

STEPHANE GRAPPELLY QUARTET   *Paris, April 10, 1956*
Stephane Grappelly (*violin*), Maurice Vander (*piano*), Pierre Michelot (*bass*), Mac Kac (*drums*)

31178	*A nightingale sang in Berkeley Square*	Barclay(F)84034, 8109213	
31179	*Body and soul*	—	—
31180	*If I had you*	—	—
31181	*I want to be happy*	—	—

84034 = Felsted(E)PDL85027 = EmArcy(US)MG36120. Title: *Improvisations*

STEPHANE GRAPPELLY AND HIS ORCHESTRA AND CHORUS   *Paris, October 2, 1956*
Stephane Grappelly (*violin*), large orchestra and chorus, Jo Boyer (*arranger, conductor*)

32798	*Pennies from heaven*	Barclay(F)82083, 820007	
32799	*Once in a while*	—	—
32800	*The very thought of you*	—	—
32801	*Yesterdays*	—	—

Same   *Paris, October 13, 1956*

32822	*Please be kind*	Barclay(F)82083, 820007	
32823	*Moonlight in Vermont*	—	—
32824	*I've got you under my skin*	—	—
32825	*Darling je vous aime beaucoup*	—	—
32826	*Lazy bones*	—	—

Same   *Paris, December 7, 1956*

33557	*Nuages*	Barclay(F)82083, 820007
33558	*Day after day*	— —
33559	*The way you look tonight*	— —
33560	*Moonglow*	— —
33561	*Ah! Que revienne*	— —

82083 = Verve MG20001 = Felsted(E)PDL85038. Title: *Musique pour Arrêter Le Temps*
820007 = Barclay 950003

STEPHANE GRAPPELLY AND STUFF SMITH   *Paris, May 4, 1957*
Stephane Grappelly/Stuff Smith (*violins*), Oscar Peterson (*piano*), Herb Ellis (*guitar*), Ray
Brown (*bass*), Jo Jones (*drums*)

21120-2	*Mean to me*	Verve unissued
21121-3	*I want to be happy*	—
21122-2	*Medley—*	—
	The nearness of you,	
	Embraceable you,	
	A nightingale sang in	
	Berkeley Square,	
	Moonlight in Vermont	
21123-1	*Don't get around much*	—
	anymore	
21124-3	*No points today*	—
21125-1	*Chapeau blues*	—
21126-2	*The lady is a tramp*	—

EDDIE BARCLAY AND HIS ORCHESTRA   *Paris, June 24, 1957*
Roger Guérin/Fred Gérarad/Maurice Thomas/Henri Vanecke (*trumpets*), Charles Huss/
André Paquinet/Benny Vasseur (*trombones*), Gabriel Vilain (*bass trombone*), Micky Nicolas/Jo
Hrasko (*altos*), Lucky Thompson/Marcel Hrasko (*tenors*), William Boucaya (*baritone*),
Raymond Guiot (*flute*), Michel Hausser (*vibes*), Art Simmonds (*piano*), Pierre Cavalli (*guitar*),
Jean Bouchety(*bass*), Kenny Clarke (*drums*), 16 strings, 8 vocalists, Stephane Grappelly
(*violin*), Quincy Jones (*arranger, director*)

| 36560 | *Tu joues avec le feu* | Barclay(F)82138 |
| 36561 | *Un p'tit bout de femme* | Barclay(F)72133, 82138 |

82138 = United Artists(F)UAL3023. LP title 82138: *Et voilà!*

Stephane Grappelli is not on other titles from this session

STEPHANE GRAPPELLY AND HIS QUARTET   *Paris, July 17, 1957*
Stephane Grappelly (*violin*), Raymond Fol (*harpsichord*), Pierre Michelot (*bass*), Allan Levitt
(*drums*)

| 36703 | *Love is back* | Barclay(F)8109213, 84066 |
| 36704 | *Jeepers creepers* | — |

Raymond Fol (*piano*), other personnel the same   *Paris, July 17, 1957*

36705	*Manoir de mes rêves*	Barclay(F)8109213, 84066
36706	*A flower is a lonesome thing*	— —
	(Strayhorn)	
36707	*It's only a paper moon*	— —

Guy Pederson (*bass*), Kenny Clarke (*drums*) replace Pierre Michelot and Allan Levitt

36746	Coquette	Barclay(F)8109213, 84066
36747	Willow weep for me	— —
36748	This can't be love	— —

Raymond Fol (*harpsichord*), other personnel the same   Paris, July 18, 1957

36749	My funny valentine	Barclay(F)8109213, 84066
36750	Blue room	— —

Raymond Fol (*piano*), Pierre Michelot (*bass*) replaces Guy Pederson   Paris, July 22, 1957

36771	Thou swell	Barclay(F)8109213, 84066
36772	By all means	— —
36773	Shine	—
36774	I found a new baby	— —

84066 = Felsted(E)PDL85060

EDDIE BARCLAY AND HIS ORCHESTRA   Paris, October 18, 1957
Probably Roger Guérin/Fred Gérarad/Maurice Thomas/Fernand Verstraete (*trumpets*), André Paquinet/Charles Russ/Benny Vasseur (*trombones*), Gabriel Vilain (*bass trombone*), Micky Nicolas/Jo Hrasko (*altos*), Don Byas/Pierre Gossez or George Grenu (*tenors*), William Boucaya (*baritone*), Raymond Guiot (*flute*), Michel Hausser (*vibes*), Art Simmonds (*piano*), Pierre Cavalli (*guitar*), Jean Bouchety (*bass*), Kenny Clarke (*drums*), Stephane Grappelly (*violin*), Quincy Jones (*arranger, director*)

238	Numero 13	Barclay unissued
239	Quincy boogie	Barclay(F)72180
240	Tout doucement	
	(add chorus)	Barclay(F)72180, 72133
241	Quelquechose en toi	Barclay(F)82128, United Artists(F)UAL3023

Stephane Grappelli is not on other titles from the above session

STEPHANE GRAPPELLY AND HIS ORCHESTRA(?)   Paris, November 13, 1957
Strings, rhythm(?), Mario Bua (*arranger*), Stephane Grappelly (*violin*)

403	Je t'aime	Barclay unissued
404	Bonsoir chérie	—
405	Je crois rêver	—
406	Rose	—
407	Puisque tu dors	—

FRANÇOIS VERMEILLE AND HIS ORCHESTRA   Paris, April 26, 1958
(*Du Rêve à la Danse*). Bernard Hulin (*trumpet*), Marcel Hrasko (*clarinet, tenor*), Michel Hausser (*vibes*), Gilbert Roussel (*accordion*), Lily Laskine (*harp*), François Vermeille (*piano, arranger*), René Duchaussoir (*guitar*), Alphonse Masseller (*bass*), Arthur Motta (*drums*), Stephane Grappelly (*violin*)

1343	Reveries	Barclay(F)82146
1344	Darn that dream	—
1345	I'll see you in my dreams	—
1346	Dream of you	—

FRANÇOIS VERMEILLE AND HIS ORCHESTRA   Paris, April 30, 1958
Bernard Hulin (*trumpet*), Marcel Hrasko (*clarinet, tenor*), Michel Hausser (*vibes*), Joss Baselli (*accordion*), Lily Laskine (*harp*), François Vermeille (*piano, arranger*), René Duchaussoir (*guitar*), Jacques Medvedko (*bass*), Arthur Motta (*drums*)

1350	A weaver of dreams	Barclay(F)82146
1351	Rêver	—
1352	De rêve en rêve	Barclay unissued

Stephane Grappelli is not on other titles from 82146. Title: *Du Rêve à la Danse*

HENRI CROLLA ALL STARS   *Paris, 1958*

Stephane Grappelly (*violin*), Hubert Rostaing (*clarinet*[1]), Andre Ekyan (*alto*[1]), René Urtreger or Maurice Vander (*piano*), Henri Crolla (*guitar*[1]), Emmanuel Soudieux (*bass*), Allan Levitt (*drums*)

Swing 39	Vega(F)V30S805, 30VT12161	
Minor swing[1]	—	—
Swing 42	—	—
Place de Brouckère[1]	—	—

Stephane Grappelli is not on other titles from the above session. Title: *Notre ami Django — Hommage de ses compagnons*

STEPHANE GRAPPELLY   *Paris, November 4, 1958*

Stephane Grappelly (*violin*), with flute, strings, chorus, Jo Boyer (*arranger*)

2147	*Begin the beguine*	Barclay unissued
2148	*My heart belongs to daddy*	—
2149	*Rosalie*	—
2150	*Easy to love*	—
2151	*Night and day*	—

STEPHANE GRAPPELLY   *Paris, November 5, 1958*

Stephane Grappelly (*violin*), flute, chorus, strings, Jo Boyer (*arranger*)

2163	*Slap that bass*	Barclay(F)80903, 82174
2164	*Nice work if you can get it*	Barclay(F)80903, 82174, 72313
2165	*What is this thing called love?*	Barclay unissued
2166	*You're the top*	Barclay unissued

As previous   *Paris, November 6, 1958*

2167	*In the still of the night*	Barclay unissued
2168	*Just one of those things*	—
2169	*The man I love*	—
2170	*Oh lady be good*	—

As previous   *Paris, November 8, 1958*

2187	*Anything goes*	Barclay unissued
2188	*Somebody loves me*	Barclay(F)80903, 82174

As previous   *Paris, November 17, 1958*

2274	*Love for sale*	Barclay unissued
2275	*All through the night*	—
2276	*It's delovely*	—
2277	*You're sensational*	—
2278	*Ça c'est l'amour*	—

As previous   *Paris, December 22, 1958*

2436	*I got rhythm*	Barclay(F)80903, 82174, BB28, 72313		
2437	*Someone to watch over me*	—	—	—
2438	*Clap your hands*	—	—	—
2439	*That certain feeling*	—	—	—

As previous   *Paris, December 23, 1958*

2440	*Love walked in*	Barclay(F)80903, 82174, BB28		
2441	*Love is here to stay*	—	—	—
2442	*A foggy day*	—	—	—	72313

As previous   *Paris, December 26, 1958*

2456	*Liza*	Barclay(F)80903, 82174, BB28			
2457	*When do we dance?*	—	—	—	72313
2458	*Summertime*	—	—	—	

As previous   *Paris, January 9, 1959*

2517	*Fascinating rhythm*	Barclay(F)80903, 82174, BB28
2518	*Somebody loves me*	Barclay unissued
2519	*Slap that bass*	—
2520	*Nice work if you can get it*	—

As previous except Raymond Guiot (*flute*) replaces unknown flute   *Paris, January 14, 1959*

2533	*Lady be good*	Barclay(F)80903, BB28	
2534	*The man I love*	—	—
2535	*You're sensational*	Barclay(F)80904	
2536	*Night and day*	—	
2537	*Just one of those things*	—	

As previous   *Paris, January 15, 1959*

2546	*What is this thing called love?*	Barclay(F)80904, 82166	
2547	*It's delovely*	—	—
2548	*Ça c'est l'amour*	—	—
2549	*I get a kick out of you*	—	—
2550	*You're the top*	—	—
2551	*Love for sale*	—	—

As previous   *Paris, January 16, 1959*

2562	*In the still of the night*	Barclay(F)80904, 82166	
2563	*Anything goes*	—	—
2564	*Begin the beguine*	—	—
2565	*Rosalie*	—	—
2566	*My heart belongs to daddy*	—	—
2567	*Easy to love*	—	—
2568	*All through the night*	—	—
2569	*Some enchanted evening*	Barclay unissued	

Title: *Stephane Grappelly plays Cole Porter.* 80904 = Felsted SPD3002

ONE WORLD JAZZ   *NYC, May 19, 1959*
Clark Terry (*trumpet*), J. J. Johnson (*trombone*), Ben Webster (*tenor*), Hank Jones (*piano*),
Kenny Burrell (*guitar*), George Duvivier (*bass*), Jo Jones (*drums*)

C063351	*Misty*[1,3]	Columbia(US)WL162, WS314, Phillips(E)BBL7361		
C063352	*International blues*[1,2,3]	—	—	—
C063354	*Nuages*[3]	—	—	—

Tapes of these titles were sent to Europe and the following musicians overdubbed their parts:

London, June 22, 1959

George Chisholm (*trombone*), Roy East (*alto*)[1], Ronnie Ross (*baritone*)[2]

Paris, July 3, 1959

Roger Guérin (*trumpet*), Bob Garcia (*tenor*), Martial Solal (*piano*)[2], Stephane Grappelly (*violin*)[3]

STEPHANE GRAPPELLY   *Paris, March 27, 1961*
Stephane Grappelly (*violin*), flute, chorus, strings, Jo Boyer (*arranger*)

7523	*Too marvellous for words*	Barclay unissued
7253(?)	*A romantic guy*	—

Stephane Grappelly (*violin*), flute, chorus, strings, Jo Boyer (*arranger*)   *Paris, April 4, 1961*

| 7307 | *Nuages* | Barclay unissued |
| 7308 | *A gal in calico* | — |

STEPHANE GRAPPELLY QUINTET   *Paris, March 7, 1962*
Stephane Grappelly (*violin*), Pierre Cavalli (*twelve string guitar*), Leo Petit (*rhythm guitar*), Guy Pederson (*bass*), Daniel Humair (*drums*)

9174	*Like someone in love*	Barclay(F)84089	
9175	*Daphne*	—	Ember(E)CJS810
9176	*You better go now*	—	

Same   *Paris, March 8, 1962*

9177	*Soft winds*	Barclay(F)84089	
9178	*Nuages*	—	
9179	*Le tien*	—	
9180	*Makin' whoopee*	—	Ember(E)CJS810
9181	*Alabamy bound*	—	

Same   *Paris, March 9, 1962*

9189	*How about you?*	Barclay(F)84089	
9190	*Django*	—	Ember(E)CJS810
9191	*Pent up house*	—	
9192	*Minor swing*	—	—

84089 title: *Django* = Barclay(F), 820105, 950080, Atlantic(US)SD1391, Everest(US)FS311. All titles except *Like someone in love* and *Pent up house* issued on London(E)SH-K8047, HA-K8047, title: *Feeling + Finesse = Jazz*

PIERRE SPIERS SEXTET with Stephane Grappelly   *Paris, 1962*
Pierre Spiers (*harp*), Stephane Grappelly (*violin*), Jimmy Gourlay (*guitar – solos*), Georges Megalos (*guitar*), Pierre Michelot (*bass*), Armand Molinetti (*drums*)

	Blue moon	Columbia(F)FP1135
	A foggy day	—
	Someone to watch over me	—
	I won't dance	—
	Deep purple	—
	Auf wiedersehen	—
	I'll remember April	—
	Over the rainbow	—
	Dinah	—

Title: *Nocturne.*

DUKE ELLINGTON'S JAZZ VIOLIN SESSION   *Paris, February 22, 1963*
Stephane Grappelly/Ray Nance/Svend Asmussen (*violins*), Duke Ellington (*piano*), Ernie Shepard (*bass*), Sam Woodyard (*drums*)

22292	*Blues in C[1]*	Atlantic(US)SD1688
22293	*In a sentimental mood*	—
22294	*Don't get around much anymore*	—
22295	*Day dreaming*	—
22296	*Cottontail*	—
22297	*Ticky's licks[1]*	—
22298	*Pretty little one[1,2,3]*	—
22299	*String along with strings[1,2]*	—
22300	*The feeling of jazz[1]*	—

22981	*Limbo jazz*[1]	—
22982	*Take the A train*	—
22983	*Passion flower*	Atlantic unissued
22984	*Volupté*	—

[1]: add Buster Cooper (*trombone*), Russell Procope (*alto*), Paul Gonsalves (*tenor*)
[2]: add Billy Strayhorn (*piano*)
[3]: omit Duke Ellington

Note: See also *Duke Ellington's Story on Records* Vol.13 1963/5 by Massagli/Volontè/Pusateri published in Italy

HUBERT CLAVECIN AND HIS RHYTHM
Paris, October 21, 1963
Stephane Grappelly (*violin*), Gérard Gustin 'Hubert Clavecin' (*clavecin*)[1], unknown flute, tenor, organ, vibes, accordion[2], piano[3], guitar, bass, drums

4447	*Hymne à l'amour*[3]	Bel Air(F)421083, 221204	
4448	*Mon légionnaire*[2,3]	—	
4449	*La vie en rose*[3]	—	—
4450	*Les trois cloches*[1,2]	—	
4451	*A quoi ça sert l'amour*[1]	—	
4452	*Milord*[1]	—	
4453	*La goualante du pauvre Jean*[1,2]	—	
4454	*Non, je ne regrette rien*	—	—

Same		*Paris, November 18, 1963*	
4557	*Padam padam*[3]	Bel Air(F)421083	
4558	*C'est d'la faute à tes yeux*[1,3]	—	
4559	*Je n'en connais pas la fin*[1,3]	—	
4560	*C'était une histoire d'amour*[1,2]	—	
4561	*C'est lui que mon coeur a choisi*[1,2,3]	—	
4562	*Mon manège à moi*[1]	—	
4563	*C'est peut-être ça*[3]	—	
4564	*J'en ai tant vu*[2,3]	—	

421083 = Bel Air(F)7007, Musidisc(F)30CV1140. Title: *Les Plus Grands Succès d'Edith Piaf*

Stephane Grappelli recorded two titles with George Daly (*vibes*) probably during 1963 in Paris
Titles: *New Cadences/Rythmes et Bergamasques* — Sonorop(F)SONO3032A

STEPHANE GRAPPELLY AND SVEND ASMUSSEN
Copenhagen, January 23/24, 1965
Stephane Grappelly (*violin*), Svend Asmussen (*violin, alto*), Ole Molim/Jorn Grauengaard (*guitars*), Neils-Henning Ørsted Pederson (*bass*), William Schiopffe (*drums*)

Honeysuckle rose	Metronome(E)MLP15177
Blue lady	—
So sorry	—
Twins	—
Satin doll	—
Love is back	—
Someone to watch over me	—
Parisian thoroughfare	—

MLP15177 = Polydor 236502 = Festival(F)JON 100019
Title: *Two of a kind*

STEPHANE GRAPPELLY AND STUFF SMITH   *Paris, June 22, 1965*
Stephane Grappelly (*violin*), Stuff Smith (*violin, vocal*), Rene Urtreger (*piano*), Michel Gaudry (*bass*), Michel Delaporte (*drums*)

15802	*This can't be love*	Barclay(F)84110
15803	*Skip it* (omit Smith)	—
15804	*Willow weep for me* (omit Grappelli)	—
15805	*Blues in the dungeon* vSS	—
15806	*S'posin'* vSS	—
15807	*How high the moon*	—

841100 = Barclay 920067 = Everest(US)FS 238

VIOLIN SUMMIT   *(?)Switzerland, September 30, 1966*
Stephane Grappelly/Stuff Smith/Svend Asmussen/Jean-Luc Ponty (*violins*), Kenny Drew (*piano*), Niels-Henning Ørsted-Pederson (*bass*), Alex Riel (*drums*)

Summit soul	Saba(G)SB15099
Pent up house[1,2]	—
It don't mean a thing	—
Pennies from heaven[1,2,3]	—
Hot toddy[1]	—

Stephane Grappelli is not on other titles from the above session. [1]: omit Stuff Smith, [2]: omit Svend Asmussen, [3]: omit Jean-Luc Ponty. SB 15009 = MPS/BASF(G)21-20626, MPS(F)15012, Prestige(US)PR7631, Polydor(E)MPS545103

VIC LEWIS AND HIS ORCHESTRA   *London, April 28, 1967*
Large concert orchestra, Stephane Grappelly (*violin*), Ken Thorne (*arranger*), Vic Lewis (*director*)

Two for the road	CBS(E)2835
Stepps	—

Note: the above 45 rpm single from the film Two For The Road

NORMANDO MARQUEZ   *Paris, 1967*
Normando Marquez (*guitar, vocal*), Stephane Grappelly (*violin*), Jean-Pierre Mongeon (*celeste*), Pierre Michelot (*bass*), Kenny Clarke (*drums*)

On a fait l'amour	Decca(F)79531
Balancon com bossa	—

Note: the above is a 45 rpm single

STEPHANE GRAPPELLI   *Paris, January, 1969*
Stephane Grappelli (*violin*), Raymond Fol (*piano*), Tony Osio (*guitar*), Jack Sewing (*bass*), André Hartmann (*drums*)

Raincheck	RCA(F)740038,	(E)INTS 1017
Camelia	—	—
I got it bad and that ain't good	—	—
What am I here for?	—	—
Tabu	—	—
Denise	—	—
Flamingo	—	—
Time on my hands	—	—
Anna	—	—
Light	—	—

Raymond Fol (*celeste*), others the same   *Paris, January 1969*

    Andrée   RCA(F)740038, (E)INTS 1017
    Zolda   —   —

Stephane Grappelli (*violin*), Raymond Fol (*celeste*)   *Paris, January 1969*

    So long   RCA(F)740038, (E)INTS 1017

RCA INTS 1017 Title: *Le Toit de Paris*

GUY MARCHAND   *Paris, February 21, 1969*
Guy Marchand (*vocal*), Stephane Grappelli (*violin*), Raymond Gimenez/Francis Lemaguer/ Didier Duprai (*guitars*), Guy Pederson (*bass*), Gus Wallace (*drums*), René Nicolas (*arranger, director*)

RV4296   *Je cherche une femme*   Riviera(F)121225, 521103

BARNEY KESSELL   *Paris, June 18, 1969*
Strings, Stephane Grappelli (*violin*), Maurice Vander (*piano*), Barney Kessel (*guitar*), Michel Gaudry (*bass*), Marcel Blanche (*drums*)

    Nuages   Mercury(F)135720MCL
    What's new?   —

Stephane Grappelli is not on other titles from the above session. LP title: *What's New?*

STEPHANE GRAPPELLI AND BARNEY KESSEL   *Paris, June 23/24, 1969*
Stephane Grappelli (*violin*), Barney Kessel (*solo guitar*), Bartholomy 'Nini' Rosso (*rhythm guitar*), Michel Gaudry (*bass*), Jean-Louis Viale (*drums*)

    I remember Django   Freedom(F)BLP30101
    Honeysuckle rose   —
    I can't get started
       (Grappelli and Kessel only)   —
    What a difference a day made   —
    More than you know   —
    Et maintenant (What now
      my love?)   —
    I found a new baby   —
    It's only a paper moon   —
    It don't mean a thing   Freedom(F)BLP30129
    Out of nowhere   —
    Tea for two   —
    Limehouse blues   —
    How high the moon   —
    Willow weep for me   —
    Little star   —
    Undecided   —
    Barniana   —

BLP30101 = Black Lion(F)BL278079, Polydor(E)2460105 *I Remember Django*
BLP30129 = Polydor(E)2460173, Black Lion(E)BLP30129 *Limehouse Blues*

STEPHANE GRAPPELLI/JOE VENUTI   *Paris, October 22, 1969*
Stephane Grappelli/Joe Venuti (*violins*), George Wein (*piano*), Barney Kessel (*guitar*), Larry Ridley (*bass*), Don Lamond (*drums*)

    I can't give you anything
      but love baby   BYG529112, Affinity(E)AFF29
    After you've gone   —   —
    Undecided   —   —
    Venupelli blues   —   —
    Tea for two   —   —

Omit George Wein
>   *My one and only love* — —

Stephane Grappelli, Joe Venuti (*violins*), George Wein (*piano*)
>   *I'll never be the same* BYG529112, Affinity(E)AFF29

AFF29 Title: *Venupelli Blues.* BYG is a German issue

STEPHANE GRAPPELLI AND GARY BURTON   *Paris, November 4, 1969*
Stephane Grappelli (*violin*), Gary Burton (*vibes*), Steve Swallow (*bass*), Bill Goodwin (*drums*)

18174	*Falling grace*	Atlantic(US)SD1597	
18175	*Here's that rainy day*	—	, SD2-321
18176	*Daphne*	—	
18177	*Blue in green*	—	
18178	*Coquette*	—	—
18179	*The night has a thousand eyes*	—	
18180	*Eiderdown*	—	
18181	*Arpège*	—	
18182	*Sweet rain*	—	

SD1597 = Atlantic(F)40378, (E)K40378
K40378 Title: *Paris Encounter*

STEPHANE GRAPPELLI   *London, June 29, 1970*
Stephane Grappelli (*violin, vocal[4]*), Marc Hemmeler (*piano[1], organ[2]*), Alan Clare (*piano[3]*), Diz
Disley (*guitar*), Lennie Bush (*bass*), John Spooner (*drums*)

I can't believe that you're in love with me[2,3]	Phillips(E)6308017
Sweet Georgia Brown[1]	—
Darling, je vous aime beaucoup[1,4]	—
Taking a chance on love[1]	—
Willow weep for me[1]	—
My one and only love[1]	—
How high the moon[1]	—
Like someone in love[3]	—
More[1]	—
I got rhythm[1]	—
Lonely Street[2]	—
The girl from Ipanema	—

All these titles on Phillips(E)6612039 (with Jean-Luc Ponty)

Title: *Stephane Grappelli and friends*

STEPHANE GRAPPELLI   *London, October 10, 1970*
Stephane Grappelli (*violin*), Alan Clare (*piano*), Kenny Napper (*bass*), Tony Crombie (*drums*)

Makin' whoopee	Pye(E)NSPL 18360,
Restless girl	— Vogue(F)DP 32
You make me feel so young	—
That tune	—

Add Marc Hemmeler (*piano*)   *London, October 10, 1970*
>   *Old man river* Pye(E)NSPL 18360, Vogue(F)DP 32

Omit Alan Clare   *London, October 10, 1970*

Peanut vendor	Pye(E)NSPL 18360, Vogue(F)DP 32	
Ain't misbehavin'	—	—
Blue river	—	
The folks who live on the hill	—	
Runnin' wild	—	
Sunny skies	—	
Passé	—	

Note: NSPL 18360 = Pye(F)SLDPY 800

NSPL 18360 Title: *Stephane Grappelli 1971*

STEPHANE GRAPPELLI   *Paris, December 13, 1970*
Stephane Grappelli (*violin*), Marc Hemmeler (*piano*), Jack Sewing (*bass*), Kenny Clarke (*drums*)

Tea for two	RCA(F)730107	
Danny boy	—	
Let's fall in love	—	
Let's fall in love	unissued	
Let's fall in love	unissued	
Coltrane	RCA(F)730107, JPGH 004	
I hear music	—	
Dany	—	FXM2-7217
Smoke gets in your eyes	—	
Gary	—	FXM2-7080
Satin doll	unissued	

Paris, December 13, 1970

Stephane Grappelli (*piano/violin*), Jack Sewing (*bass*), Kenny Clarke (*drums*)

Dear Ben	RCA(F)730107

Stephane Grappelli (*violin*), Kenny Clarke (*piano*)   *Paris, December 13, 1970*

Body and soul	RCA(F)730107

Paris, December 13, 1970

Stephane Grappelli (*piano*), Marc Hemmeler (*organ*), Jack Sewing (*bass*), Kenny Clarke (*drums*)

A flower for Kenny	RCA(F)730107
A flower for Kenny	unissued

730107 = RCA(E) SF8184 = INTS 5047 = CL37197 A/B (part of double LP No. CL37197 Title *In Paris*). CL37197 is a French issue

Title: *I hear music* (INTS5047, 730107, SF8184)

STEPHANE GRAPPELLI   *Villengen, March, 1971*
Stephane Grappelli (*violin*), Marc Hemmeler (*piano*), Eberhard Weber (*bass*), Kenny Clare (*drums*)

This can't be love	MPS/BASF(G)21-20876-1
Time after time	—
Undecided	—
You were only passing by	—
Tangerine	—
Chicago	—
Manoir de mes rêves/Daphne	—
Misty	—
Afternoon in Paris	—
Autumn leaves	—

20876 = BAP5001, MPS(F)15066, 75004, (G)68156, Pausa(US)7071. Title: *Afternoon in Paris*

STEPHANE GRAPPELLI AND GÉRARD GUSTIN   *Paris, 1971*
Stephane Grappelli (*violin*) with large string orchestra directed by Gérard Gustin

Acajou	unissued
Astéroide	—
Astronef	—
Autoroute du sud	—
Corail	—
Direction uranus	—
Équinoxe	—
Étoile de mer	—
Gamma	—
Grande ourse	—
Metéorite	—
Mimétisme	—
Orbite	—
Satellite	—
Toi l'albatros	—
Utopie	—
Zénith	—

PAUL SIMON   *Paris, 1971*
Stephane Grappelli (*violin*), Paul Simon (*guitar, vocal(?)*)

Hobo's blues	CBS(F)S69007

STEPHANE GRAPPELLI   *London, November 8, 1971*
Stephane Grappelli (*violin*), Alan Clare (*piano*), Lennie Bush (*bass*), Terry Jenkins (*drums*)

How about you	Pye(E)NSPL18374, (F)SLDPY844	
Someone to watch over me	—	—
This can't be love	—	—
The nearness of you	—	—
Nuages	—	—
Lady be good	—	—
Mean to me	—	—
Manoir de mes rêves	—	—
Daphne	—	—
Sweet Georgia Brown	—	—
I can't give you anything but love baby	—	—

NSPL18374 Title: *Stephane Grappelli 1972*

All the above titles on Vogue(F)DP32

STEPHANE GRAPPELLI AND YEHUDI MENUHIN   *London, June 14, 1972*
Stephane Grappelli/Yehudi Menuhin (*violins*), Alan Clare (*piano*), Lennie Bush (*bass*), Chris Karan (*drums*), Max Harris (*arranger, conductor*)

The blue room	EMI(E)EMD5504
A fine romance	—
Love is here to stay	—
Pick yourself up	—

The same   *London, June 15, 1972*

Jealousy	EMI(E)EMD5504, UV2
Night and day	—

Omit Menuhin   *London, June 15, 1972*

Billy	EMI(E)EMD5504

Yehudi Menuhin(*violin*), Stephane Grappelli (*piano*) *London, June 15, 1972*

    Aurore   —

EMD5504 = Angel(F)SEO36968 = EMI-VSM(F)2C064-02446

UV2 = sample disc (?)*The present life*(?)

EMD5504 Title: *Jealousy – Hits of the 'thirties.* See March 1973 for further titles on EMD5504

STEPHANE GRAPPELLI *London, June 19, 20, 21 and 22, 1972*

Stephane Grappelli (*violin*), Alan Clare (*piano*[1], *electric piano*[2]), Marc Hemmeler (*piano*[3], *electric piano*[4]), Ernie Cranenburgh (*guitar*), Lennie Bush (*bass*), Chris Karan (*drums*)

Sweet Sue[3]	Festival(F)Album 120,	
Avalaon[3]	—	Visadisc V1326
Manoir de mes rêves[4]	—	Musidisc(F)30CV1285
Clopin-clopant[1]	—	Visadisc V1326,
		Musidisc(F)30CV1285
Daphne[1]	—	—
Blues[1]	—	
Swing guitar[1]	—	—
I wonder where my baby is tonight[1]	—	
Djangology[1]	—	—
Swing 39[1]	—	—
Oriental shuffle[2]	—	
Minor swing[4]	—	
Venez donc, chez moi[2]	—	—
I saw stars[1]	—	
Fantaisie[1]	—	
Dark eyes[1]	—	—
I'm coming Virginia[3]	—	
I'll remember April[1]	—	—

Stephane Grappelli (*piano*), Alan Clare (*piano*) *London, June 19–22, 1972*

    Are you in the mood?   Festival(F)Album 120, Visadisc V1326

Stephane Grappelli (*violin*), Alan Clare (*electric piano*) *London, June 19–22, 1972*

Tears	Festival(F)Album 120,	
Sweet chorus	—	
Nuages	—	Visadisc V1326

Note: Album 120 = Classic Jazz(US)CJ23, Musidisc(F)CCV2520 (part of a four album set)
Title: *Hommage à Django Reinhardt*

STEPHANE GRAPPELLI *Paris, November 12/13, 1972*

Stephane Grappelli (*violin*), Eddie Louiss (*organ*)[1], Marc Hemmeler (*piano*)[2], Jimmy Gourley (*guitar*)[3], Guy Pederson (*bass*), Kenny Clarke (*drums*)

Satin doll[1,2]	Festival(F)FLD596, Musidisc(F)CCV2520	
On the sunny side of the street[2]	—	
Body and soul (1st)[2,3]	—	
Ain't misbehavin'[2,3]	—	
Mack the knife[1,2,3]	—	—
Body and soul (2nd)[1]	—	
Pennies from heaven[1,2]	—	
The girls from Ipanema[1,2,3]	—	
Blue moon[2,3]	—	

The lady is a tramp[1,2]	—	—
Exactly like you[2]	—	—
Ebb tide[1]	—	
You took advantage of me[2,3]	—	
Lover man[2,3]	—	
I didn't know what time it was[3]	—	
Hallelujah[1,2]	Festival(F)FLD629	

Stephane Grappelli (*violin*), Eddie Louiss (*organ*)   *Paris, November 12/13, 1972*

     My funny valentine   Festival(F)FLD596, Musidisc(F)CCV2520

As last, add Kenny Clarke (*drums*)   *Paris, November 12/13, 1972*

     In a mellow tone   Festival(F)FLD596

FLP596 is a double LP, title *Satin Doll*

SACHA DISTEL   *Paris, 1972*
Sacha Distel (*vocal, guitar*), Stephane Grappelli (*violin*), orchestra directed by Gérard Gustin

     Ma première guitar   EMI Pathé(F)2C006-93878

STEPHANE GRAPPELLI – OSCAR PETERSON QUARTET   *Paris, February 22/23, 1973*
Stephane Grappelli (*violin*), Oscar Peterson (*piano*), Neils-Henning Ørsted-Pederson (*bass*),
Kenny Clarke (*drums*)

Them there eyes	America(F)30AM6129,	
Flamingo	—	
Makin' whoopee	—	Musidisc(F)CCV2521
Looking at you	—	
Walking my baby back home	—	
My one and only love	—	
Thou swell	—	
I won't dance	America(F)30AM6131	
Autumn leaves	—	
My heart stood still	—	
Blues for Musidisc	—	
If I had you	—	
Let's fall in love	Festival(F)FLD629	
Time after time	—	

Stephane Grappelli (*violin*), Oscar Peterson (*piano*)   *Paris, February 22/23, 1973*

     The folks who live on the hill   America(F)30AM6131

30AM6129 and 6131 = Prestige(US/F)PR24041 (double album)

STEPHANE GRAPPELLI   *London, February/March 1973*
Stephane Grappelli (*violin*), Alan Clare (*piano*), Lennie Bush (*bass*), Tony Crombie (*drums*)

It don't mean a thing	Pye(E)NSPL18403, Vogue(F)DP32	
I've got the world on a string	—	
What are you doing the rest of my life?	—	
The birth of the blues	—	—
Opportunity	—	
Just a gigolo	—	—
Didn't we?	—	
Crazy rhythm	—	—
It might as well be Spring	—	—
Three little words	—	—
Avalon	—	

Stephane Grappelli (*piano*)   *London, February/March 1973*

       Emotion   Pye(E)NSPL18403

NSPL18403 = Vogue(F)LDM30210
Title: *Stephane Grappelli 1973*

STEPHANE GRAPPELLI AND YEHUDI MENUHIN   *London, March 6, 1973*
Stephane Grappelli/Yehudi Menuhin (*violins*), Alan Clare (*piano*), Ken Baldock (*bass*), Tony
Crombie (*drums*), Max Harris (*arranger, conductor*)

       I can't believe that you're in
         love with me   EMI(E)EMD5504
       These foolish things   —
       Lady be good   —

Yehudi Menuhin (*violin*), Stephane Grappelli (*piano*)   *London, March 6, 1973*

       Jermyn Street   EMI(E)EMD5504

As previous   *London, March 7, 1973*

       Cheek to cheek   EMI(E)EMD5504
       The lady is a tramp   —

Omit Menuhin   *London, March 7, 1973*

       Erroll   —

EMD5504 Title: *Music of the 'thirties Vol. 1*
EMD5504 = Angel SE036968 = EMI-VSM(F)2C064-02446

STEPHANE GRAPPELLI   *Denham, England, March 19, 1973*
Stephane Grappelli (*violin*), Alan Clare (*piano, celeste*)

       The talk of the town   Black Lion(E)BLP30165,
       Amada   —   SAM20130
       Starous   —
       Can't help lovin' that
         man o' mine   —
       We'll be together again   —
       Nature boy   —
       The nearness of you   —
       Tournesol   —
       Greensleeves   —
       You go to my head   —

BLP30165 Title: *The talk of the town* = Black Lion(US)BL313

HERBIE MANN   *USA(?), March(?) 1973*
Herbie Mann (*flute*), Stephane Grappelli (*violin*), Pat Rebillot (*keyboard*), Albert Lee (*guitar*),
Al Gorry (*bass*), Aynsley Dunbar (*drums*)

27914   *Mellow yellow*   Atlantic(US)SD1648

Stephane Grappelli is not on other titles from the above session

TRIANGLE-HOMONYMIE   *Paris, March/April 1973*
Stephane Grappelli (*violin*), François Jeanneau (*keyboard*), Marius 'Mimi' Lorenzini (*guitar*),
René Devaux (*bass*), Jean-Pierre Prévotat (*drums*)

       Éloge de la folie   Pathé(F)2C062-12493

STEPHANE GRAPPELLI   *Montreux, July 4, 1973*
Stephane Grappelli (*violin*), Marc Hemmeler (*piano*), Jack Sewing (*bass*), Daniel Humair
(*drums*)

Just one of those things	Black Lion(E)BLP30152,	2460213
Misty	—	—
More	—	—
Que reste-t-il de nos amours?	—	—
Don't get around much anymore	—	—
Them there eyes	—	—
Honeysuckle rose	—	—
All God's chillun got rhythm	Black Lion(E)BLP30148,	—

Stephane Grappelli (*violin*), Barney Kessel (*guitar*)   *Montreux, July 4, 1973*

Tea for two	Black Lion(E)BLP30148,	2460213

BLP30152 = Freedom(F)BLP30152 = Black Lion(US)BL211 all titled: *Just one of those things*
Also = BLP12183 Title: *In Concert*

BLP30148 = Black Lion(US)BL213 Title: *Black Lion at Montreux*

Stephane Grappelli does not perform on the other titles on BLP30148

STEPHANE GRAPPELLI   *London, September 5, 1973*
Stephane Grappelli (*violin*), Roland Hanna (*piano and electric piano*), George 'Jiri' Mraz (*bass*),
Mel Lewis (*drums*)

Perugia	Black Lion (E)BLP30183
Fascinating rhythm	—
Parisian thoroughfare	—

Same   *London, September 7, 1973*

Love for sale	Black Lion(E)BLP30183
Two cute	—
Improvisation on prelude in E Minor	—
Wave	—
Hallelujah	—

Same sessions

Nice work if you can get it	Black Lion(F)157002
Shangri-la	—
Two cute	—

BLP30183 Title: *Stephane Grappelli meets the rhythm section*
BLP30183 = Arista/Freedom(US)1033 Title: *Parisian*

STEPHANE GRAPPELLI   *London, November 5, 1973*
Stephane Grappelli (*violin*), Diz Disley/Denny Wright (*guitars*), Len Skeat (*bass*)

This can't be love	Black Lion(E)BLP30158,	2683047
I can't believe that you're in love with me	—	—
Misty	—	—
After you've gone	—	—
Manoir de mes rêves/Daphne	—	—
Satin doll	Black Lion(E)BLP30159	—

Tea for two	—	—
Flamingo	—	—
Honeysuckle rose	—	—
Nuages	—	—
Sweet Georgia Brown	—	—
Gershwin Medley		
(Summertime, But not for		
me, I got rhythm)	—	—

The above taken from a concert at The Queen Elizabeth Hall, London

Title: *I got rhythm*

STEPHANE GRAPPELLI *Paris, December 3/4, 1973*
Stephane Grappelli (*violin*), Bill Coleman (*trumpet, cornet or flugel*), Marc Hemmeler (*piano*),
Guy Pederson (*bass*), Daniel Humair (*drums*)

I've got the world on a string	Festival(F)Album 155, Classic Jazz(US)CJ24	
St Louis blues	—	—
Ain't she sweet?	—	—
Moonlight in Vermont	—	—
Stardust	—	—
Where or when	—	—
S'wonderful	—	—
Chicago	—	—

Omit Bill Coleman *Paris, December 3/4, 1973*

Summertime	Festival(F)Album 155
Lullaby of birdland	—
After you've gone	—
Sweet Georgia Brown	—
Three little words	—
All the things you are	—
Fly me to the moon	—

JEAN-LUC PONTY/STEPHANE GRAPPELLI *Paris, December 27, 28, 29, 1973*
Jean-Luc Ponty (*violin,*[1] *baritone violin,*[2] *arranger, composer*), Stephane Grappelli (*violin,*[3]
baritone violin[4]), Maurice Vander (*piano, electric piano*[5]), Philippe Catherine (*guitar*), Tony
Bontils (*bass*), André Ceccarelli (*drums*)

Bowing bowing[1,3,5]	America(F)30AM6139
Golden green[2,3,5]	—
Memorial jam for	
Stuff Smith[1,3,5]	—
Violin summit No.2[2,3,6]	—
Valerie[1,4,6]	—

30AM6139 = Inner City(US)IC1005

LES VALSEUSES *Paris, January 4/5, 1974*
Stephane Grappelli (*violin, composer*), Maurice Vander (*organ,*[1] *keyboard,*[2] *piano*[3]), Marc
Hemmeler (*piano*[4]), Philippe Catherine (*guitar*[5]), Guy Pederson (*bass*), Daniel Humair (*drums*)

Ballade[1,5]	Festival(F)FLD629
Jeanne 1[1,5]	—
Jeanne 2[1]	—
Rolls 1[2]	—
Poursuite[4,5]	—
Rolls 2[3]	—

Maurice Vander (*organ, plus keyboard dubbed*), Marc Hemmeler (*piano*), Philippe Catherine (*guitar*), Guy Pederson (*bass*), Daniel Humair (*drums*), Stephane Grappelli (*composer*)

Ballade	Festival(F)FLD629

STEPHANE GRAPPELLI AND EARL HINES

London(?), July 4, 1974

Stephane Grappelli (*violin*), Earl Hines (*piano*)

Fine and dandy	Black Lion(E)BLP30193
Over the rainbow	—
Manhattan	—
Moonlight in Vermont	—
I can't get started	—
You took advantage of me	—
Sometimes I'm happy	—

Title: *The Giants*

STEPHANE GRAPPELLI AND BADEN POWELL

Paris, September 4/5, 1974

Stephane Grappelli (*violin*), Baden Powell (*guitar*), Guy Pederson (*bass*), Pierre Alain Dahan (*drums*), Jorge G. Rezendre/Clement De Waleyne (*percussion*)

Eu vim de bahia	Festival(F)FLD634
Meditacao	—
Berimbau	—
Desafinado	—
Samba de una nota so	—
Isaura	—
Amor em paz	—
Brazil	—
The girl from Ipanema	Festival(F)FLD642
Waves	—
Ingenuo	—
O pato	—
Rancho fundo	—
Blues samba	—
Peanut vendor	—

Note: LP FLD642 has not been released to date

STEPHANE GRAPPELLI AND THE DIZ DISLEY TRIO

Villingen, Germany, March, 1975

Stephane Grappelli (*violin*), Diz Disley/Ike Isaacs (*guitars*), Isla Eckinger (*bass*)

Lover come back to me	MPS/BASF(G)20-22545-3,	(E)BAP5063,	Pausa(US)7098
Sweet Lorraine	—	—	—
Shine	—	—	—
Solitude	—	—	—
Ain't misbehavin'	—	—	—
Souvenir de Villingen[1]	—	—	—
Hot lips	—	—	—
My heart stood still	—	—	—
The nearness of you	—	—	—
Joy	—	—	—
A nightingale sang in Berkeley Square	—	—	—
Cherokee	—	—	—
Lover man	—	—	—

Title: *Violinspiration*

Note: [1]Stephane Grappelli overdubbed piano and violin

STEPHANE GRAPPELLI AND SLAM STEWART
Paris, March 25, 1975

Stephane Grappelli (*violin*), Johnny Guarnieri (*piano*), Jimmy Shirley (*guitar*), Slam Stewart (*bass, vocal*), Jackie Williams (*drums*)

–1 *I would do anything for you*	Black & Blue	(F)33076
–2 *I would do anything for you*	—	unissued
–1 *'Deed I do*	—	—
–2 *'Deed I do*	—	(F)33076
–1 *As time goes by*	—	—
–2 *As time goes by*	—	unissued
–1 *You're the cream in my coffee*	—	(F)33076
–1 *It's only a paper moon*	—	—
–2 *It's only a paper moon*	—	unissued
–1 *You're driving me crazy*	—	—
–2 *You're driving me crazy*	—	(F)33076
–1 *It had to be you*	—	—
–2 *It had to be you*	—	unissued
–3 *It had to be you*	—	—
–1 *My blue heaven*	—	—
–2 *My blue heaven*	—	(F)33076
–1 *I'll never be the same*	—	unissued
–1 *Autumn in New York*	—	—
–1 *But not for me*	—	—
–2 *But not for me*	—	—

Stephane Grappelli (*piano solos*)
Paris, March 25, 1975

[1]*Sysmo*	Black & Blue	unissued
[2]*Sysmo*	—	(F)33076
[1]*Flonville*	—	—
[2]*Flonville*	—	unissued

Title: *Steff and Slam*

CAROLINE CLER/CHRISTIAN BOREL
Paris, April 19, 1975

Stephane Grappelli (*violin*), strings, piano, electric piano[2], guitar, bass, drums, Caroline Cler/ Christian Borel (*vocals*), Lucien Lavoute (*arranger, director*)

Sur deux notes vCC	Musidisc(F)30CV1350
Bonsoir chérie vCB	—
Queresté de nous amours? vCB	—
Il ne faut pas buser un rêve[2] vCC	—

Brass replace strings
Paris, April 19, 1975

Chez moi vCC	Musidisc(F)30CV1350
Cheveux dans le vent vCB	—

Stephane Grappelli does not play on other titles from the above session
LP title: *Amour Toujours*

PIERRE ET LE LOUP
Paris(?), 1975

Stephane Grappelli (*violin*), Alvin Lee (*guitar*)[1], Dave Marquee (*bass*)[2], Pierre Clementi (*narrator*)

Cat dance[1,2]	RSO(US)SO1812,	(F)2479168
Cat[2]	—	—
Cat in tree	—	—

Stephane Grappelli does not play on other titles from the above session

STEPHANE GRAPPELLI/YEHUDI MENUHIN   *London, May 21, 1975*
Stephane Grappelli/Yehudi Menuhin (*violins*), Denny Wright/Ike Issacs (*guitars*), Lennie
Bush (*bass*), Max Harris (*arranger, conductor*)

      Just one of those things   EMI(E)EMD5523
      Fascinating rhythm   —
      Liza   —
      I got rhythm

Stephane Grappelli (*violin*), Ike Isaacs (*guitar*)   *London, May 21, 1975*

      Johnny aime   EMI(E)EMD5523

                                          London, May 22, 1975
Stephane Grappelli/Yehudi Menuhin (*violins*), Alan Clare (*piano*), Ike Issacs (*guitar*), Lennie
Bush (*bass*), Ronnie Verrell (*drums*), Max Harris (*arranger, conductor*)

      I get a kick out of you   EMI(E)EMD5523
      Soon[1]   —
      S'wonderful[1]   —

Yehudi Menuhin (*violin*), Stephane Grappelli (*electric piano*)   *London, May 22, 1975*

      Minuet pour Menuhin   EMI(E)EMD5523

Omit Ike Isaacs, Alan Clare (*electric piano*)[2]   *London, May 23, 1975*

      Summertime[2]   EMI(E)EMD5523
      Nice work if you can get it[1] —
      Looking at you   —
      Embraceable you   —
      Why do I love you?   —
      All the things you are[1]   —

[1]Max Harris (*piano*) may replace Alan Clare on these titles
EMD5523 = EMI-VSM(F)2C064-02690. LP title: *Music Of The Thirties, Vol. 2*
EMD5523 Title: *Fascinatin' rhythm*

STEPHANE GRAPPELLI   *Paris, May 26–27, 1975*
Stephane Grappelli (*violin*), Marc Hemmeler[1], Maurice Vander[2] (*piano*), Eddie Louiss
(*organ*)[3], Ike Issacs (*guitar*)[4], Luigi Trussardi (*bass*)[5], Daniel Humair (*drums*)[6]

      That certain feeling[1,3,5,6] Festival(F)Album 205
      I got plenty of nuttin'[2,3,5,6] —
      *They can't take that away from
        me*[3]   —   Musidisc(F)CCV2520
      But not for me[1,5,6]   —
      The man I love[1,3,4,5,6]   —   —
      Somebody loves me[2,4,5,6] —
      Do do do[2,3,5,6]   —
      It's all right with me[1,3,5,6] Festival(F)Album 240   —
      Anything goes[2,3,5,6]   —
      You've got a thing[3,5,6]   —
      *I've got you under my
        skin*[1,3,5,6]   —
      Love for sale[3]   —   —

STEPHANE GRAPPELLI   Paris, February 2–3, 1976
Stephane Grappelli (*violin*), Maurice Vander (*piano*)[1], Eddie Louiss (*organ*)[2], Jimmy Gourly
(*guitar*)[4], Guy Pederson (*bass*)[4], Daniel Humair (*drums*)[5]

Clap your hands[1,2,3,4,5]	Festival(F)Album 205	
A foggy day[1,2,3,4,5]	—	Musidisc(F)CCV2520
I was doing all right[2,3,4,5]	—	
How long has this been going on?[2,3,4,5]	—	
They all laughed[1,2,4,5]	Festival(F)Album 240	
You're the top[2]	—	
In the still of the night[1,2,3,4,5]	—	—
Miss Otis regrets[2]	—	
Easy to love[1,3,4,5]	—	—
You'd be so nice to come home to[2,3,4,5]	—	
My heart belongs to Daddy[1,2,4,5]	—	

Titles: *Stephane Grappelli plays George Gershwin* (205), *Cole Porter* (240)

STEPHANE GRAPPELLI AND GEORGE SHEARING   Villengen, April 11, 1976
Stephane Grappelli (*violin*), George Shearing (*piano*), Andrew Simpkins (*bass*), Rufus Jones
(*drums*)

I'm coming Virginia	MPS(G)68162
Time after time	—
La chanson de rue	—
Too marvellous for words	—
It don't mean a thing	—
Makin' whoopee	—
After you've gone	—
Flamingo	—
Star eyes	—
The folks who live on the hill	—

Title: *The Reunion*

JEAN SABLON   Paris, December 13, 1976
Stephane Grappelli (*violin*), Maurice Vander (*piano*), Luigi Trussardi (*bass*), Daniel Humair
(*drums*), Jean Sablon (*vocal*)

Tout seul	Festival(F)Album 259
Oui je m'en vais	—
Tu sais	—
La dernière chanson	—

Stephane Grappelli does not play on other titles from the above session

STEPHANE GRAPPELLI   Paris, February 17/18, 1977
Stephane Grappelli (*violin*),Eddie Louiss (*organ*), Pierre Michelot (*bass*), Daniel Humair
(*drums*)

All God's chillun got rhythm	Festival(F)FLD673	
Deliciosa[1]	—	
Blue skies	—	
Gravenstein	—	
A Stephane	—	
Stormy weather[1]	—	Musidisc(F)CCV2520
Sing for your supper	—	

[1] Stephane Grappelli (*piano and violin*) dubbed

Title: *Stephane Grappelli and Eddie Louiss*

122

Stephane Grappelli (*violin*), Don Burrows (*clarinet*[1], *flute*[2], *bass flute*[3], *alto*[4]), George Golla
(*guitar*)

A fine romance[1]	Cherry Pie(Au)CPF1032
Don't get around much anymore[2]	—
I can't get started[1]	—
Autumn leaves[1]	—
I'll never be the same	—
Down home blues[1]	—
I only have eyes for you/Shine	
Solitude[3]	
Corcovado[4]	—
It's only a paper moon[4]	—

Title: *Steph 'n' us*

STEPHANE GRAPPELLI   *Paris, June 1977*
Stephane Grappelli (*violin*) with unknown vibes, guitar, bass, drums, directed by Camille
Sauvage

Leasing	Timing(F)15DWS LP3357
Brett	—
Jessie	—
Whist	—
Story	—
Tric-trac	—
Pearl	—
Paganini	—

Stephane Grappelli (*violin*) and overdubbed electric piano[1], piano[2]   *Paris, June 1977*

Kindness[1]	Timing(F)15DWS LP3357
Jerome[2]	—
Gina[1]	—
Amaud[2]	—

Title: *Grappelli plays Grappelli*

Stephane Grappelli (*violin*), Maurice Vander (*piano, electric piano*[1]), Gérard Wiobey (*guitar*),
Tony Bonfils (*bass*), André Ceccarelli (*drums*), François Jeanneau (*synthesizer*), Michel
Delaporet (*percussion*), large concert orchestra, Christian Chevalier (*arranger, director*)

You are the sunshine of my life	Festival(F)FLD685
Jeanne	—
Berimbau	—
Fumette[1]	—
Bill	—
Yesterday	—
Michelle	—
Baratana[1]	—
Ballade	—
Recado	—
Elé[1]	

Title: *Stephane Grappelli and Strings*

STEPHANE GRAPPELLI   *Amsterdam, October 28/29/30, 1977*
Stephane Grappelli/Yehudi Menuhin (*violins*) with Laurie Holloway (*keyboards*), Pierre
Michelot (*bass*), Ronnie Verell (*drums*)[2], John Etheridge/Jan Block (*guitars*), Pierre Michelot
(*bass*), Ronnie Verell (*drums*)[1], and unknown woodwinds/reeds[4]

Viva Vivaldi[2,4]	EMI(E)EMD5530
Air on a shoe string[2,4]	—
The man I love[2,4]	—
Thou swell[2,4]	—
Crazy rhythm[1]	—
Limehouse blues[1]	—
Between the devil and the deep blue sea[1]	—
Tea for two[1]	—
Yesterdays[2]	—
My funny Valentine[2]	—
A foggy day[2]	—

Stephane Grappelli (*piano*), Yehudi Menuhin (*violin*)   *Amsterdam, October 28–30, 1977*

Highgate Village	EMI(E)EMD5530
Adelaide Eve	—

EMD55530 = VSM(F)2CO64-02997 = Angel(US)S37533.

One title, *I didn't know what time it was*, remains unissued from one of the above sessions

STEPHANE GRAPPELLI   *NYC, March 1978*
Stephane Grappelli (*violin*), Jimmy Rowles (*piano*), Jay Berlinger (*guitar*), Ron Carter (*bass*),
Grady Tate (*drums*), strings, Aaron Rosand (*concert master*), Claus Ogerman (*arranger,
conductor*)

Baubles, bangles and beads	Columbia(US)JC35415, CBS(E)82959	
Angel eyes	—	—
Favors	—	—
A waltz dressed in blue	—	—

                                                                  NYC, 1978
Stephane Grappelli (*violin*), Richard Tee (*electric piano*), Hugh McCracken (*guitar*), Anthony
Jackson (*bass*), Steve Gadd (*drums*), Rubeus Bassini (*conga, percussion*), strings, Aaron Rosand
(*concert master*), Claus Ogerman (*arranger, conductor*)

Pages of life	Columbia(US)JC35415, CBS(E)82959	
Uptown dance	—	—
Smoke rings and wine	—	—
Shadows	—	—
Nightwind	—	—

Title: *Uptown Dance*

STEPHANE GRAPPELLI   *Brignoles, July 17, 1978*
Stephane Grappelli (*violin*), Roland Hanna (*piano*), Bucky Pizzarelli (*guitar*), George Duvivier
(*bass*), Oliver Jackson (*drums*)

The lady is a tramp	Black & Blue(F)33132
Sweet chorus	—
Let's fall in love	—
Sweet and lovely	—
Tears	—
Louise	—
Stray horn	—

Title: *Stephane Grappelli and his American friends*

DAVE GRISMAN   *NYC(?) 1978*
Stephane Grappelli (*violin*), Dave Grisman/Mike Marshall (*mandolin*), Tony Rice (*guitar*),
Eddie Gomez (*bass*)

> *Minor swing*   Horizon(US)HP731
> *16–16*   —

Stephane does not play on other titles from the above session

Title: *Hot Dawg*

STEPHANE GRAPPELLI QUARTET   *Stuttgart, January 19/21, 1979*
Stephane Grappelli (*violin*), Philip Catherine/Larry Coryell (*guitars*), Niels-Henning Ørsted-
Pedersen (*bass*)

> *Djangology*   MPS(G)68230, Pausa(US)7041
> *Sweet chorus*   —   —
> *Minor swing*   —   —
> *Are you in the mood?*   —   —
> *Galerie St. Hubert*   —   —
> *Tears*   —   —
> *Swing guitars*   —   —
> *Oriental shuffle*   —   —
> *Blues for Django and*
> *   Stephane* (Stephane —   —
> *   Grappelli* piano also)

Title: *Young Django*

STEPHANE GRAPPELLI   *Copenhagen, Denmark, July 6, 1979*
Stephane Grappelli (*violin*), Joe Pass (*guitar*), Niels-Henning Ørsted Pedersen (*bass*)

> *It's only a paper moon*   Pablo-Live 2308220
> *Time after time*   —
> *Let's fall in love*   —
> *Crazy rhythm*   —
> *I'll remember April*   —
> *I can't get started*   —
> *I get a kick out of you* —

Stephane Grappelli does not play on the one other title from the above LP — *How deep is the
ocean?*. LP recorded in concert at Tivoli Gardens Copenhagen. Title: *Stephane Grappelli/Joe
Pass/Niels-Henning Ørsted Pedersen*

STEPHANE GRAPPELLI   *Copenhagen, Denmark, July 6, 1979*
Stephane Grappelli (*violin*), Joe Pass (*guitar*), Niels-Henning Ørsted Pederson (*bass*), Micky
Roker (*drums*)

> *Nuages*   Pablo-Live 2308232
> *How about you?*   —
> *Someone to watch over me* —
> *Makin' whoopee*   —
> *That's all*   —
> *Skol blues*   —

LP recorded in concert at Tivoli Gardens, Copenhagen. Title: *Skol*

STEPHANE GRAPPELLI/BUCKY PIZZARELLI   *Nice, France, July 15, 1979*
Stephane Grappelli (*violin*), Bucky Pizzarelli (*guitar*)

> *There's a small hotel*   Ahead(F)33755
> *Tangerine*   —
> *My blue heaven*   —

The folks who live on the hill   —
Alabamy bound   —
Willow, weep for me   —
Blues   —
Have you met Miss Jones?   —
My one and only love   —
I'll remember April   —
Black bottom   —
This nearly was mine   —

Title: *Duet*

STEPHANE GRAPPELLI & HANK JONES   *London, July 20, 1979*
Stephane Grappelli (*violin*), Hank Jones (*piano*), Jimmie Wood (*bass*), Alan Dawson (*drums*)

Thou swell   String(F)33852
These foolish things   —
September in the rain   —
You better go now   —
Hallelujah   —
Yesterday   —
Mellow grapes   —
I'll never be the same   —

Note: Bass and drums do not perform on *These foolish things*. LP Title: *London meeting*

STEPHANE GRAPPELLI/DAVE GRISMAN   *Boston, USA, September 20, 1979*
Stephane Grappelli (*violin*), Dave Grisman (*mandolin*), Mike Marshall (*mandolin, guitar*[1]),
Mike O'Connor (*guitar, violin*[1]), Tiny Moore (*electric mandolin*)[2], Rob Wasserman (*bass*)

Sine[1]   Warner Brothers(G)WB56903
Pent up house   —
Misty   —
Sweet Georgia Brown   —
Tiger rag   —
Swing '42   —
Medley (Tzigani, Fizztorza,
    Fulginiti)   —
Satin doll[2]   —

Note: *Satin doll* recorded in San Francisco September 7, 1979

Title: *Live*

WB560903 = Warner Brothers(US)BSK3550, (F)WE351

STEPHANE GRAPPELLI QUARTET   *Nice, France, December 20/21, 1979*
Stephane Grappelli (*violin*), Gérard Gustin (*piano*), Jack Sewing (*bass*), Armand Cavallaro
(*drums*)

Bélier   Blue Silver(F)BS3002
Gémeaux   —
Lion   —
Balance   —
Sagitiaika   —
Verseau   —
Taureau   —
Cancer influence   —
Vierge   —
Scorpion   —
Capricorne   —
Poissons   —

Title: *Stephane Grappelli '80*

Stephane Grappelli (*violin*), Martial Solal (*piano*)   *Paris, February 17/18, 1980*

Shine	Owl(F)021
Valsitude	—
Sing for your supper	—
God bless the child	—
Nuages	—
Parisian thoroughfare	—
Grandeur et cadence	—
Stumbling	—
Et so l'on improvisait?	—

Title: *Happy Reunion*

Nice, France, February 28/29, 1980

Stephane Grappelli (*violin*), Gérard Gustin (*piano*), Jack Sewing (*bass*), Armand Cavallaro (*drums*)

Saluting Basie	Blue Silver(F)BS3007
Portrait of Jobim	—
Oscar	—
Dedicated to Joao	—
Fats delight	—
Kenny's tune	—
To Django	—
Tribute to The Bird	—
Remembrances to Duke	—
Ode to Ray Brown	—
Dizzy	—
To Benny	—

BS3007 = Europa(US)JP2001. Title: *Stephane Grappelli 'Tribute to'*

STEPHANE GRAPPELLI   *London, April 6/7, 1980*

Stephane Grappelli (*violin*), Elena Duran (*flute*), Laurie Holloway (*keyboards*), Allen Wally (*bass*), Allan Ganley (*drums*)

Brandenburg boogie	EMI(E)EMD5536,	Angel(US)DS37790
Jesu, joy of man's desiring	—	—
Groovy gavotte 1	—	—
Fascinating fugue	—	—
Groovy gavotte 2	—	—
Sleepers awake	—	—
Aria	—	—
D Minor double	—	—
Minuet	—	—
Jig	—	—
Air on a G string	—	—
Groovy gavotte 3	—	—
Sicilienne	—	—
Funky flute	—	—

Title: EMD5536, DS37790 = *Brandenburg boogie*

STEPHANE GRAPPELLI   *Saratoga, Ca., September 1980*

Stephane Grappelli (*violin, electric viola*), John Etheridge/Martin Taylor (*guitars*), Jack Sewing (*bass*)

You are the sunshine of my life	Concord(US)CJ139
Love for sale	—
Angel's camp	—
Willow, weep for me	—
Chicago	—
Taking a chance on love	—

Minor swing	—
Let's fall in love	—
Just you, just me	—

Title: *Stephane Grappelli at the Winery.*

STEPHANE GRAPPELLI   *London, early 1981*
Stephane Grappelli (*violin*), Elena Duran (*flute*), Laurie Holloway (*piano, arranger*), Allan
Walley (*bass*), Allan Ganley (*drums*)

Yesterday	RCA(E)LP6007
All my loving	—
Eleanor Rigby	—
Norwegian wood	—
Can't buy me love	—
Here, there and everywhere	—
Michelle	—
Hey Jude	—
The long and winding road	—
A hard day's night	—

Title: *Norwegian Wood.*

STEPHANE GRAPPELLI   *London, May 1, 1981*
Stephane Grappelli (*violin*), Martin Taylor/Diz Disley (*guitars*), Jack Sewing (*bass*)

I'm coming, Virginia	Wave, unissued
Mean to me	—
Swing '42	—
Makin' whoopee	—
Do you know what it means	—
(to miss New Orleans)	
Crazy Rhythm	—
You're driving me crazy	—
A foggy day	—
If I had you	—
Manhattan Tea party	—

STEPHANE GRAPPELLI   *San Francisco, July 1981*
Stephane Grappelli (*violin*), Mike Gari/Martin Taylor (*guitars*), Jack Sewing (*bass*)

Blue moon	Concord(US)CJ 169
It's only a paper moon	—
I'm coming Virginia	—
I can't get started	—
Do you know what it means	
to miss New Orleans?	—
But not for me	—
If I had you	—
Isn't she lovely?	—

Stephane Grappelli (*fender rhodes*), Martin Taylor (*guitar*)   *San Francisco, July 1981*

Jamie	Concord(US)CJ169

Title: *Vintage 1981.*

STEPHANE GRAPPELLI/YEHUDI MENUHIN WITH NELSON RIDDLE

London, July 15, 1981

Stephane Grappelli/Yehudi Menuhin (*violins*), Derek Watkins/Derek Healey/one unknown (*trumpets*), Don Lusher/two unknown (*trombones*), Roy Willox/Bill Skeat/two unknown (*woodwinds, reeds*), four french horns, ten violins, eight celli, three violas, David Snell (*harp*), Laurie Holloway (*keyboards*), Martin Taylor (*guitar*), Niels-Henning Ørsted Pedersen (*bass*), Allan Ganley (*drums*), Derek Price (*percussion*), Nelson Riddle (*arranger, conductor*)

Putting on the Ritz	EMI(E)EMD5539, Angel(US)DS37860	
The way you look tonight	—	—
Change partners	—	—
Top hat	—	—
The continental	—	—
The carioca	—	—
The piccolino	—	—

Stephane Grappelli/Yehudi Menuhin (*violins*), Ray Swinfield (*flute*), Laurie Holloway (*keyboards*), Martin Taylor (*guitar*), Eddie Tripp (*bass*), Allan Ganley (*drums*), Derek Price (*percussion*), Nelson Riddle (*arranger, conductor*)   *London, July 16, 1981*

He loves she loves	EMI(E)EMD5539, Angel(US)DS37860	
Isn't this a lovely day?	—	—
They can't take that away from me	—	—
Funny face	—	—
They all laughed	—	—

Stephane Grappelli (*piano*), Yehudi Menuhin (*violin*)   *London, July 1981*

Alison	EMI(E)EMD5539, Angel(US)DS37860	
Amanda	—	—

STEPHANE GRAPPELLI/MARTIN TAYLOR   *London, July 1981*
Stephane Grappelli (*violin*), Martin Taylor (*guitar*)

She's funny that way	EMI(E)EMD5540
Don't get around much anymore	
Manhattan Tea party	—
Here there and everywhere	—
I can't believe that you're in love with me	—
Ol' man river	—
It had to be you	—
I've got the world on a string	—
Medley: Mémoires de mes rêves/Daphne	—

Stephane Grappelli (*piano*)   *London, July 1981*

Je n'sais plus	EMI(E)EMD5540

INDEX
Illustrations in bold type